"Do You Understand What You Are Reading?"

A Presbyterian Primer

"DO YOU UNDERSTAND WHAT YOU ARE READING?"
Acts 8:30 ESV

Kenneth A. Pierce
Robert H. Miller

Metokos Press
Narrows, VA 24124

© 2006 by Metokos Press.

All rights reserved. Written permission must be secured from the publisher, Metokos Press, to use or reproduce any part of this book, except for brief quotation in critical reviews or articles. Contact Metokos Press at 211 Main Street, Suite 108, Narrows, VA 24124.

Unless otherwise indicated, all Scripture quotations are from The Holy Bible, English Standard Version, copyright 2001 by Crossway Bibles, a division of Good News Publishers. Used by permission. All rights reserved.

Published by Metokos Press, Inc., committed to providing materials easily accessible to the average reader while at the same time presenting biblical truth from within the framework of biblical and confessional churches of Reformed and Presbyterian heritage. Visit us on the web at www.metokospress.com.

Cover design by Chip Evans, Walker-Atlanta, Atlanta, GA.

Layout and editing by Diane Hitzfeld, Crestview, FL.

Printed in the United States by Lightning Source, LaVergne, TN.

ISBN 978-0-9742331-8-5

Introduction to the Series

Presbyterian Primers is a series of medium-length books, written in a non-academic style that I hope will be accessible to the many people (but especially "guys") in churches who do not regularly read books about "church stuff."

Since my seminary days, I have frequently complained that, in arenas other than Reformed and Presbyterian circles, one could find many books written in such a manner. But the majority of Reformed and Presbyterian related works were either designed as adult Sunday school textbooks (with the expectation of a certain level of understanding that goes with such readers), or were written by academics with the hope that fellow academics and a few academically minded people would buy enough copies to cover the cost of publication. There has seldom been literature designed more specifically to reach new or previously unread church members on topics of importance.

The series will include a growing but not fixed number of titles. Volumes on *Biblical Church Government, God the Holy Spirit, The Historical Roots of the Presbyterian Church in America, New Geneva Introduction to the Old Testament,* and *New Geneva Introduction to the New Testament* are already in print. After this volume on biblical interpretation, others may include titles such as *God the Father, God the Son,* an introductory (but not systematic) work on the Westminster Confession entitled *Conversations on the Confession,* and perhaps others.

Foreword

Ken Pierce and Bob Miller have done us a favor. They have given ministers and Bible teachers an accessible, easy to read, understand and digest tool to teach our people how to study the Bible for themselves. This is important and helpful at a number of levels. It is important because of the dismaying biblical illiteracy of members of Christian churches. They need to be helped in understanding both the form and content of Scripture if they are going to grow. This little book will give ready aid on that count. It is important because good Bible preaching will help people to learn how to read the Bible for themselves. But in our day, we have to teach people how to listen to expositional messages, as well as train faithful ministers how to preach expositionally. This book will help in the former, and thus aid those trying to do the latter. It is important because "hermeneutics" often presents us with large, overwhelming, indigestible volumes that are difficult to break down into a usable form for a congregation. This book's simplicity and clarity, however, make it a candidate for many uses in the local church or school. It could also easily form the outline of a Sunday school course or Bible class, function as a part of an officer or leadership training curriculum, be used by small groups, or in a number of other Christian educational contexts. Take it. Read it. And benefit. I already have!

Ligon Duncan
Senior Minister, First Presbyterian Church
Jackson, MS

Acknowledgements

To Dr. Don Clements, at whose behest I wrote, because of his ardent passion to equip a knowledgeable eldership to serve and grow Christ's church, to Dr. Bob Miller, because he is a stellar example of an elder thus equipped, and to those noble Bereans of Draper's Valley Presbyterian Church who both hunger to have the Word rightly divided to them, and desire to learn how to divide it rightly for themselves.

Kenneth Pierce
Draper, VA
June 2006

To my wife, Beverly, in appreciation of her 58 years of loving care, I dedicate my work on this book.

Robert Miller
Blacksburg, VA
June 2006

Contents

Getting Started: Principles and Tools 1

Christian at the Interpreter's House 17

God's Story: Historical Narrative 35

"Why the Law, Then?" 47

Lovelier Than Trees: Poetry in the Scriptures 63

For Crying Out Loud: Wisdom in the Bible 77

"Thus Says the Lord": The Prophets 93

God Became Man: The Gospels 107

"Dear Christian": The Epistles 119

Behold, He Is Coming: The Revelation 131

About the Authors 143

Chapter One
Getting Started: Principles and Tools

The Bible is the word of God: no more, no less. This is one of the foundational principles of Evangelical Christianity. Indeed, it was one of the foundational principles of the Protestant Reformation. This principle is very well stated in the Westminster Confession of Faith, chapter 1, paragraph 6: "The whole counsel of God, concerning all things necessary for his own glory, man's salvation, faith, and life, is either expressly set down in Scripture, or by good and necessary consequence may be deduced from Scripture: unto which nothing at any time is to be added, whether by new revelations of the Spirit, or traditions of men."

The Bible is no less than the word of God. As our Confession states, it is the *whole* counsel of God. Nothing is to be added to it. To amend the Scripture by adding anything to it, no matter how reasonable the addition might seem to us, would be to adulterate the word of God. That would be placing our own fallible, limited wisdom above the infallible, infinite wisdom of God, who gave us his word. This seems obvious. It is something which none of us would dare to do deliberately. But even though none of us would ever dare to cut out words or pages and insert our own ideas, we have to be careful not to do that in a less obvious way by reading our own ideas or traditions into the words of Scripture. That is something very easy to do inadvertently, and the avoidance of it is one of the main objects of this study.

The Bible is no more than the word of God. That is, all of it is God's word to us. In reaction to the liberalism of the Enlightenment, the Neo-Orthodox theologians tried to bring back respect for the Bible by saying, "The Bible contains the word of God," but they didn't go far enough. While that statement is true, it is not the whole truth. The entire Bible is God's word. It contains God's word in the same way a water bottle completely full to the brim contains water. As Paul tells us (or should we say "as God tells us"?) in 2 Timothy 3:16 (KJV), "All scripture is given by inspiration of God, and is profitable..." Now, it has to be acknowledged that using Scripture to prove the divine inspiration of Scripture is circular reasoning. It is not a proof in the sense of formal logic, but it is a powerful support of our faith as we approach Scripture with the presupposition that it is completely and entirely God's word.

One way in which this principle of looking at the Bible as being completely God's word to us has been expressed has been to affirm its *plenary, verbal* inspiration: *verbal*, because the words themselves were inspired by God; *plenary*, because all of them were completely inspired. None of the passages of the Bible are to be considered something placed there by the writer out of his own mind without having been written under the inspiration of God.

Consider, for a moment, the consequences of holding a lesser opinion of the Bible. If it contained some portions that were not inspired, and therefore not necessarily true, how would we know which parts to believe? When we read, "For by grace are ye saved through faith," how would we know whether or not to believe it? Thus, any lesser opinion of the inspiration of Scripture destroys its effectiveness in the very heart of its function—that is, in being the basis of our faith.

It would seem that an acceptance of the principle that the Bible is the word of God would make the matter of biblical interpretation almost trivial. After all, we can read what it says, and believe it, so what's the problem? Well, the problem is that many people have done this, and they have come up with many different understandings of the meaning of the same passage of Scripture. That's one of the reasons it is of such importance to be careful and methodical in our study of the word, to be sure that the message we perceive is truly the message God has given.

There are several reasons why a surface reading of a passage might cause us to misunderstand what God is saying. Let's consider a few of them.

Language. Obviously, the Bible was not written in English. The Old Testament was written mostly in Hebrew, with a few portions being written in Aramaic, a closely related language. Both of these languages differ from English, not only in the words used to express an idea, but also in the alphabet and even in some of the grammatical construction. The New Testament was written in Greek. This language is much closer to our own. But still, many of the words are different (although many of our words have Greek roots), the alphabet is different (although much closer to our own), while the grammatical construction is much closer to that of English.

Not many of us are Hebrew or Greek scholars. That means we have to rely on others to do the translating. Fortunately, there are plenty of people who have done this work for us. (Some might say there are too many translations available.) Yet we still are left with a problem, since the translations differ from one another, sometimes significantly. These differences are due to several factors.

First, language is imprecise. For example, when we use the word "letter", we might mean one of the characters which make up our words. Or we might mean a written message. Or again, we might mean an exact interpretation ("the letter of the law"). We could even mean proficiency in the arts (a "man of letters") or an athlete who has lettered in a sport. In any language, most words have a range of meaning. If the ranges were identical in the different languages, this would not be much of a problem; but the ranges overlap. A word in the original language might have a range of meaning that could translate into any of several different words in English. Only the context can indicate which choice would be most accurate, and not all translators always agree.

But the problem gets worse. Today's English is a far cry from the 17th century English of the King James translation. For example, 2 Thes. 2:7 (KJV) says, "...He who now letteth will let..." This expression means almost the opposite to us now. The more modern statement would be, "...He who now restrains will restrain..." The English of 2006 is even different from that of 1940, when a computer was a person who sat at a desk doing calculations. This is one of the main reasons for the large number of new translations.

Culture. We live in a technological society. This is becoming true even in the third world. Our culture is far different from the agrarian and sometimes nomadic society of Biblical times. Even if we could arrive at a perfect translation of a particular sentence, there is such a cultural difference involved that the sentence could impress different images on our minds than it did to the Israelites. For example, Ps. 33:17 (KJV) tells us, "An horse is a vain thing for safety: neither shall he deliver any by his great strength." Most of us know from history what this is saying but there are very few of us who can remember when the cavalry consisted of horse-mounted troops. Some translators might even go so far as to change the words to "A tank is a vain thing..." but this is a dangerous approach to the problem. Not only will tanks one day be obsolete, but such tinkering with the words could easily reach the point of destroying "plenary, verbal inspiration".

Genre. The reader may have noticed that the Table of Contents lists chapters on different genres or types of passages in Scripture: narrative, prophecy, epistles, etc. There is a reason why this book deals with these types of passages separately. Each genre is written for a specific purpose to a specific audience or readership. It is only to be expected that the style, vocabulary, even the figures of speech would vary. We don't go to the historical books to find doctrinal teaching. We find very little poetry in the Epistles. It is necessary, therefore, to know what to look for in each type of biblical writing, and to be acquainted with the interpretive methods specific to each genre.

Manuscript evidence. It would be wonderful if we had in our possession the original letter that Paul wrote to the believers at Ephesus, or even a reliably exact copy. The same could be said of most passages of Scripture. But we don't have that. We have many ancient copies and fragments of copies in various libraries around the world, which have been preserved and sorted and classified and studied. These copies show an amazing degree of agreement, but they do not agree in every detail. They reflect copyists' errors (in the days before the printing press). They even contain occasional "corrections" of the sort suggested in the previous paragraph concerning horses. (This is the reason for the authors' disapproval of such modern "clarifications" in the text itself.)

But cheer up. All is not lost. None of these discrepancies has an effect on any essential doctrine of our faith. In fact, it is only rarely that one has any effect at all on even minor doctrines. Still, when we are trying to determine as accurately as possible exactly what God has told us in his word, it is necessary to try to resolve these differences. This is the aim of the science of Textual Criticism. This discipline seeks to reconstruct, as nearly as possible, the original language of Scripture. One of the tools of this effort is the dating, as nearly as possible, the manuscripts that are studied. Older manuscripts tend to be more exact than later ones. Another, even more powerful tool is the sorting and classifying of manuscripts into a sort of family tree, according to their variations. In this way, even a more recent manuscript might be shown to be free of errors, which had originated earlier. But, let us repeat, none of these variations has a serious enough effect on our understanding of the Scriptures to cause us undue concern.

In addition to these problems which are largely external to the reader, and in which most of us have to rely on the expertise of trained linguists and scholars, there are problems with our own efforts and attitudes that need to be recognized and avoided.

Context. With the possible partial exception of the book of Proverbs, all scriptural statements are written within the context of a larger paragraph or section. They can rarely be isolated and understood correctly without reference to this context. Probably the best example of the need for considering the context is the fictional story of Joe, who began each day by choosing a verse at random to be God's message to him for the day. One day, his random choice fell on Matt. 27:5 (KJV),

"And he cast down the pieces of silver in the temple, and departed, and went and hanged himself." That didn't seem to be too meaningful for the day, so Joe took another random choice. This time, it fell on Luke 10:37 (KJV), "…go, and do thou likewise." Poor Joe!

The idea of context will be stressed throughout this book. One of the main causes of error in our understanding of Scripture is the failure to consider context.

Presupposition. It is easy to take for granted that we know what a particular passage means. After all, there are things which many of us have been taught since childhood concerning God, his Son Jesus, and his Church. We have heard these things so often that we simply accept them as truth. In most cases, they are. But that is not always the case. When we come to the Scriptures, our purpose is to receive God's message. In order to do that, we must be sure that we do not read our own ideas into the Scripture. As we said above, to do this is to add to Scripture, at least mentally.

Scripture interprets Scripture. One of the primary principles to guide us in our biblical interpretation and to protect us from the difficulties and pitfalls listed above is the principle that Scripture interprets Scripture. Historical context or literary context may help us greatly in our understanding. Attention to genre is important. But none of these things can ever override the principle that we must not understand one passage in such a way that it would contradict another passage dealing with the same subject in the same context. This principle will be discussed in more detail in the next chapter.

So that is a rather imposing list of difficulties which we might face in our effort to understand the biblical message. But don't lose heart. The tools and resources available to us are sufficient to enable us to realize the joy of hearing for ourselves (through spiritual ears) God's word. Every bit of time and effort devoted to this end will be abundantly rewarded in a deeper understanding of God's grace. Let's take a look at these tools.

Bibles. Obviously, the first resource needed for the practice of biblical interpretation is a Bible. In fact, it is advisable to have two or more versions. The comparison of a passage between two or more translations can alert us to differences that need to be examined carefully.

The King James Version of the Bible has been known and loved for many generations. Most of the scriptural quotations in our culture, literature and history have been taken from this version. The language used, although largely obsolete, is truly beautiful, even poetic. The fact that the language is not our everyday way of speaking helps many people in memorizing verses or passages. For these reasons, it is an excellent source for devotional reading. However, in addition to the language problem, it has a serious flaw with respect to use in serious biblical interpretation. It is based on the Greek source known as the *Textus Receptus*. In the year 1611, when this translation was originally completed (it has been revised twice), this was the best source known. Subsequent manuscript discoveries and analysis have given modern translators a much more reliable picture of the original text of Scripture. Therefore, for serious exegetical study, a newer version is better.

One concern in the choice of translations for serious study is the question of the approach that the translators have used in their work. The Bible presents to us a message from God. This message consists of ideas. These ideas are expressed in words. The translator is faced with the choice of translating the words as accurately as possible (verbal or formal equivalence), or expressing the ideas in what he believes to be the most accurate way (functional equivalence). It is the opinion of the authors that the most useful translations for serious study are those that most closely follow the original words. This is somewhat loosely called a verbal translation.

Do You Understand What You Are Reading?

The New American Standard Bible (NASB) is a modern English version that has made a deliberate effort to be verbally consistent with the original manuscripts. When such a verbal translation is likely to cause confusion in the mind of the reader, a necessary change has been made in the text, with a marginal note alerting the reader. Occasionally, a word will be added for clarity. Such a word is italicized to indicate that it was not in the original language. We strongly recommend this translation.

Another translation which has followed a pattern of verbal equivalence is the English Standard Version (ESV). The New International Version (NIV) has almost as consistently followed a pattern of verbal equivalence. Either or both of these translations is reliable for studying, as nearly as possible, the original word.

A good study Bible will contain several study helps. The most common consists of marginal notes, either cross-referencing words or subjects with other biblical occurrences or offering an alternate translation. More thoroughly annotated Bibles will often contain notes giving an explanation of a passage as a commentary would. Many will contain an introduction to each Book, giving an outline and possibly giving background information concerning the historical circumstances of its writing. Many study Bibles contain an index, which greatly assists a topical study. They may also contain a concordance (usually abbreviated) to assist the reader in finding other significant occurrences of a particular word. Finally, many study Bibles will contain a set of maps of Bible lands and periods, perhaps with a gazetteer (an index of places on the maps). These are all features that can assist in our study of the Bible itself. Two outstanding study Bibles are (1) The Reformation Study Bible, edited by R. C. Sproul and Keith Mathison, published by Ligonier Ministries, Orlando, Florida, (an ESV translation), and (2) Spirit Of The Reformation Study Bible, edited by Richard L. Pratt, Jr., et al, published by Zondervan, Grand Rapids, Michigan (an NIV translation).

One other Bible resource is a good electronic version for installation on a personal computer. There are many commercial versions, many including several translations along with search features and one or more commentaries. One good source is found at FreeBibleSoftware.com. Their Bible Study Library contains several translations of the Bible, together with several commentaries and maps. An electronic version of the New American Standard Bible or the English Standard Version, together with helps, can be found at most Bible bookstores, either retail or on-line.

Commentaries. Next to the Bible itself, a good commentary, or even two, is the greatest resource in biblical interpretation. While it is true that a commentary is the work of a man or men, and it is not inspired, it remains a tremendous help in our understanding of the word. Although we cannot simply read a commentary and assume that we understand exactly what the Bible is teaching in a given passage, it would be foolish to cast aside the insight of great Bible scholars of the past (whose work has stood the test of time) or even of the present.

Several recommended works would be the New Bible Commentary (Davidson, Stibbs and Kevan) or, for a set, the Eerdmans/IVP Tyndale Old Testament and New Testament Commentaries.

A good commentary will usually include an introduction to each Book of the Bible, which will not only give an outline of the book, but, when appropriate, some information concerning the history, culture, or special problems of the country or city involved.

Concordance. Many Bibles contain a concordance, citing the occurrences of many key words. A more complete concordance, such as Strong's or Young's, is a great help in finding, through undertaking a word search, parallel passages which can shed light on the passage under study. Of course, it is necessary that the concordance be keyed to the version of the Bible that one is using in his study. Many electronic Bibles will have a search function, which can do the job more quickly, and can be searched by phrase as well as by word.

In using any of these resources (other than the biblical text itself), one should remember that they are not inspired documents as are the original Scriptures. Some are unduly influenced by denominational distinctives. It is essential to continue to think for oneself. If it were otherwise, there would be no need for a course in biblical interpretation. At the same time, we should give due respect to these aids, as many are produced by great men of God who have devoted much of their lives to such study and teaching.

Note: Most lay students of the Bible would probably not wish to devote the effort to become somewhat familiar with the original languages, but a resource which one of the authors (not a seminary graduate) has found very helpful in finding shades of meaning from the original language of the New Testament is an Interlinear Greek New Testament (such as G. R. Berry, Zondervan, which describes manuscript variations and includes a lexicon). Perhaps a lexicon (such as F. W. Gingrich, U. of Chicago), and a very elementary Greek grammar (such as A Beginner's

Do You Understand What You Are Reading?

Reader-Grammar for New Testament Greek, by E. C. Colwell and E. W. Tune, Harper & Row) would be advantageous. One may not become a Greek Scholar through the use of such resources, but with grammar charts found in the book, it is surprising how quickly one can develop the ability to appreciate (with some diligence) more fully what the scriptural writer says. Still, the fact remains that good Bible interpretation can be done without these resources.

Chapter Two
Christian at the Interpreter's House

Then Christian began to gird up his loins, and to address himself to his Journey. So the other told him, that by that he was gone some distance from the Gate, he would come at the house of the interpreter, at whose door he should knock, and he would shew him excellent things.   John Bunyan, *The Pilgrim's Progress*

There is a true story about a student who had the privilege of studying under the noted Harvard biologist Louis Agassiz. He arrived at the laboratory, and the noted professor placed in front of him a preserved fish. "Study this fish," Agassiz said, "and record your findings." The professor soon left, and the student began observing the fish. The next day, the student reported his finding to Agassiz. The same scene repeated itself this day, "Study this fish, and record your findings." Again and again, day after day, the assignment was the same. Soon, the student grew tired of the exercise. But, then, after several days, he began to notice things about the fish he had never seen before—he simply had not known how to look carefully enough. That was the point of the exercise—biology was about, in the first place, thorough and careful examination.

That is the task of the Bible interpreter. We may glean precious truths upon a casual or devotional read of the Scriptures. But, the closer and more careful our study, the more accurate and profound our insights will be. And, the more we learn to avoid common mistakes in interpretation, the more true our teaching will be to the Word that we seek faithfully to proclaim.

This chapter serves as an introduction to the basic rules and cautions of biblical interpretation. The application of these rules, with examples of them, will follow in subsequent chapters. Many of the principles enumerated in this chapter are further explained in R. C. Sproul's excellent book, *Knowing Scripture*.

There are three levels to the interpreter's task: observation, interpretation, and application. These must be undertaken in order, and each one is very important. There is no doubt that most mistakes in interpretation and application come because the foundation of observation has been inadequately laid, or not laid at all. It is always tempting to skip the first two difficult tasks (observation and interpretation) and immediately begin to apply the Scriptures, which appears more relevant and gratifying. This we must not do. After all, our goal, in the first place, is to find out what the Scriptures teach, not to imagine how what *we think* they teach applies to our lives.

Observation. The first level of biblical interpretation is observation (exegesis). This is the all-important job of discovering what the text actually says, and it is not as easy as it at first appears. Careful study of things such as the meanings of words (determined by use of the dictionary), how the same words function in other contexts, the grammatical construction and emphases, all come into play at this level. It may appear intimidating at first, but it is a learned skill, and there are ample helps available to those willing to seek them out.

It must be noted, too, that in observation, one must be careful to "read out of" a text what is there, and not "read into" a text something one presumes is there, but is not. An example: Jesus said, "It is easier for a camel to go through the eye of a needle than for a rich person to enter the kingdom of God." (Matthew 19:24). Some think the Needle's Eye was a low gate into the city of Jerusalem, and for camels to go through, they had to be unburdened of all their worldly baggage. Therefore, if rich people would enter the kingdom, they must unburden themselves of all their worldly baggage. An utterly fetching illustration? Maybe, but it is also utterly false. It is an imposition on the text. First, there is no evidence of the existence of such a gate. Even if there were, there is no evidence that this is what Jesus had in mind. It is "knowledge" from an outside source used to interpret a passage. This is sometimes referred to as *eisegesis*, or "reading into" a text. It is far better to look at the context, and see that the disciples understood very well what Jesus was saying, exclaiming, "Who then can be saved?" (Matthew 19:25) Jesus responds with the point, "With man this is impossible, but with God all things are possible." (Matthew 19:26) The point of Jesus' illustration is very clear—it is not that the salvation of a rich man is hard, although he can attain it by unburdening himself of his possessions; it is, rather, that it is impossible for anyone, rich young ruler or poor disciple, to save themselves; God must do it.

Examples of this type of "reading in" could be multiplied. Another example: in 1 Corinthians, Paul argues that women ought to worship and pray with their heads covered, and that women ought not to have shorn heads. We are often told it was customary in ancient Greco-Roman society for women to cover their heads, that those who went about with brazenly uncovered heads were prostitutes, and those whose heads were shorn were temple prostitutes. True? Maybe. But, again, it is an imposition on the text. Whatever argument we may make for allowing women to have uncovered heads in worship, we ought not to make it because of an understanding of ancient Greco-Roman culture. After all, this same argument is often alleged against upholding biblical roles for men and women in the home and church, and the impropriety of homosexuality. The argument from cultural factors ought never be allowed to muzzle the word of God, and what it commands us to do, and not do.

It is here that the importance of context and type of literature comes into view. Looking at context saves us from a world of interpretive mistakes. How many people will assert, in favor of women's ordination that, "There is neither Jew nor Greek, there is neither slave nor free, there is neither male nor female, for you are all one in Christ Jesus." (Galatians 3:28) But, is Paul addressing the question of leadership there? If he is, he is woefully inconsistent with his other statements, such as 1 Timothy 2:12, "I do not permit a woman to teach or to exercise authority over a man; rather, she is to remain quiet." It is clear, from reading the rest of Galatians 3 and 4 that Paul's concern here is not the relative roles of men and women in the church, but rather that all persons, whether Jew, Greek, slave, free, men and women are saved in the same way, not by works or by birth, but by faith in Christ.

How to read in context. If one is to teach a lesson or preach a sermon, how does one choose a text? This will vary depending on the type of literature from which the text is chosen, but always ought to be a smaller or larger coherent paragraph or thought unit. Even if the text proper is only one or two verses, the method is the same. The text under consideration should be viewed as the center point of your study.

First, determine, insofar as you can, what the point of the text is, in a preliminary way. This may have to be revised as you examine context. Then, look at the thought units immediately surrounding it. How does it function within that larger section? Modern translations have a wonderful tool to help you do this, and that is the dividing of the text into paragraphs. But, it must be remembered that paragraphs, like verse and chapter numbers, and even punctuation, are not original to the text, and are based on the interpretation of translators and editors.

It is a helpful exercise to write out a one-sentence summary of the several preceding paragraphs, and following paragraphs, to see how the verses under consideration fit in the overall scheme of the author's argument. Then, look at the overall book. It is helpful to read the entire book of the Bible through twice, and maybe even develop a simple outline of the concerns and major ideas of a book.

If these tasks seem daunting, a study Bible is an invaluable tool. The best study Bibles have outlines and introductions at the beginning of each book, which will help you see how each section functions in the context of the whole book. There is also usually a summary of what the book is about, when it was written, who wrote it, and the situation of the audience to whom it was written. All of this will help you determine what is actually being said.

But, there is even more to be considered, and more help available. It is of great help to consider the historical context of a passage or book. Ideally, one might do this from the text itself. but a reliable study Bible will also aid one in answering simple questions about the particular book. When was it written? By whom? To whom? Where? What was the cultural situation of those to whom it was written? What was going on in the world around the recipients to which the book speaks?

This is of enormous help, especially when it comes to reading prophecy correctly. What was looming in the future of God's people when Amos prophesied? Does it make a difference that Haggai prophesied after the return of Judah from exile?

These types of questions help us shape our understanding of what the text says.

Interpretation. The second stage of biblical interpretation is interpretation proper (hermeneutics). It is here that we seek to understand the meaning of the ancient texts. If observation is concerned with what the text *says*, interpretation is concerned with what the text *means*. While specific examples will follow, there are basic principles that universally hold true in Bible interpretation.

The cardinal rule of Bible interpretation is the *analogy of faith*, or the belief that "Scripture interprets Scripture." The Westminster Confession, I.9, states, "The infallible rule of interpretation of scripture is the scripture itself; and therefore, when there is a question about the true and full sense of any scripture (which is not manifold, but one) it must be searched and known by other places that speak more clearly."

It is important to note this full explanation. The Confession explains that the Bible interprets itself. If there are two possible interpretations of a particular passage, and one is in harmony with what is taught in the rest of Scripture, that interpretation is to be preferred. For example, James 2:24 states, "You see that a person is justified by works and not by faith alone." Many people have been stymied by how to reconcile that verse with the clear teaching of Paul (and Jesus) that a man is not justified by his works, else he would have something to boast about, but rather by faith apart from works. The analogy of faith helps us here. Considered in its immediate context, there are two possible interpretations of James's words: (1) A person is truly justified by God by works. (2) True and saving faith that justifies always shows itself in works. How would one decide between the two interpretations? According to the analogy of faith, the latter interpretation is to be preferred, because it comports with the rest of Scripture.

The Confession also states that, when one is confronted with an obscure verse, one that is difficult to interpret, such verses are to be read in light of passages whose truth is clear. Certainly, such things may involve an interpretive judgment—after all, what is confusing to one person may be clear to another. Yet, a helpful thing to remember is that all the doctrines of the Scripture are taught in more than one place. If one devises a doctrine purely upon one verse of Scripture, and can find no other support for it anywhere else in the word of God, such a doctrine is mistaken.

One thinks, in this regard, of the teaching of some churches that baptism must be in the name of Jesus only (not the Trinity), and that baptism actually remits sin. This doctrine rests solely upon Acts 2:38, despite the other numerous examples of Trinitarian baptism found in the Scriptures.

But, there is more to the analogy of faith. The analogy of faith teaches us that, though the Bible is made up of many books of diverse kinds, it tells one story, the story of redemption. The Bible begins with the beginning of history, and ends with the end of history. Its climax is the dividing point of history: the cross and the empty tomb. Thus, in all of our biblical interpretation, whether from Leviticus or Luke, we are to keep our eyes on the central message of the Scripture: the message of God's creation, mankind's fall into sin and condemnation, the redemption freely offered in Christ, and the consummation of all things when Christ comes to judge the living and the dead, and institutes the New Heavens and the New Earth. In other words, all passages are to be read in the light of Christ and the Gospel. This is not always an easy thing to discover, and yet it is central to the interpreter's task.

There is still one more principle to derive from the analogy of faith, and that is that the whole Scripture is to be read from the perspective of the New Testament. As Christians, we enjoy the fullness of God's revelation, the complete picture, and the fulfillment of all God planned to do in the person of Jesus Christ. As Hebrews 1:1-2 states, "Long ago, at many times and in many ways, God spoke to our fathers by the prophets, but in these last days he has spoken to us by his Son, whom he appointed the heir of all things, through whom also he created the world." Jesus, his death, resurrection, ascension and imminent return form the completion of God's revelation. Thus, in one sense, we read the Bible back to front. Or to put it another way, we are to read the Old Testament in light of the New Testament. This principle will be more fully explained in the portion of this book that discusses prophetic books, but helps us to understand what we are to expect in terms of the fulfillment of biblical prophecies.

The second major principle of interpretation is that the Bible is to be read according to its *plain (or literal) sense*. We are not to seek hidden meanings in the Scripture, in mystical codes beneath the text or in the numbers within the text. What it meant to its original hearers, it means to us. That principle may seem clear enough, and yet, through so much of church history, the clear teaching of Scripture was hidden under fanciful interpretations.

Every Scripture had four levels of meaning. For instance, Sproul notes that when the Scriptures mention Jerusalem, the obvious sense was that it meant "the capital of Israel," then Judah and Judea. But, the second or "moral" sense was "the human soul." The allegorical meaning was "the church," and the anagogical meaning was "heaven." It is clear that such a method opens the text up to say whatever strikes one's fancy. This is not to say that the Scripture doesn't use metaphor and imagery to convey truths but that, when it does so, such is clearly indicated by the context.

The method of interpretation propounded by the Reformers, especially Calvin, is known as the *grammatical-historical method*. It simply means this: we are to approach the Scriptures according to the rules of grammar and the historical contexts in which they were written. In short, the Scriptures are to be read like any other work of human language, even though its contents are divinely inspired and therefore inerrant. God communicated in language, and according to normal patterns of speech and understanding. The Bible is not a puzzle whose intention is to keep God hidden, but a revelation whose purpose is that God may be understood.

Yet, at the same time, we must be clear about what reading the Scriptures literally means. For a century and a half, the principle of strict literalism has had major play in American evangelicalism, and it has led to much confusion. Some dispensationalists stressed that all prophesies must have literal, exact, one-to-one fulfillments, that the Scriptures were to be read through the lens of the Old Covenant, and that the teachings of the New Testament must be fit into the mold of the Old Testament, not vice-versa. Therefore, God must have two eternal peoples, Israel and the church, with two distinct sets of promises, earthly and heavenly, and never the two shall meet. Since the Sermon on the Mount was spoken to Israel in the age of Law, it could not be applied directly to the church as a rule of Christian life.

What we are propounding is a more common sense approach. We are to read the Scriptures asking not only the question, "What do they say?" but "What did the authors mean?" For purposes of interpretation, we must insist that the intent of God in each Scripture is one and the same with the intention of the human author. The meaning of Scripture to us is the same as it meant to its original audience. These principles, though they require more work from the interpreter, will save us from a multitude of mistakes in interpretation.

At this point, you are probably sensing the enormity of the interpretive task. Don't be discouraged. Like all worthwhile pursuits, knowing, understanding, and applying the Bible requires effort, but it is an acquired skill. The more one does it, the more confident one will become. (It is important never to become over-confident, and forsake the fundamental skills of the task.)

Some have said that biblical interpretation is more art than science. That is true, as long as one remembers that true art follows certain acquired techniques and skills, even as it calls forth from the artist creativity and attention to detail, with an eye to making an accurate rendering of the original subject. Biblical interpretation is such an art.

Application. The third step in the task is application. This is an important step, and it is one that distinguishes the Bible from all other reading. One doesn't pick up a novel, and then ask the question, "What does this novel tell me about how to live my life?" The Scriptures are a covenant document, offered to us by God. Thus, they call forth from us a faithful response.

Moreover, it is here one bridges the gap from the ancient text and the ancient setting to contemporary life. What does the commandment, "Thou shalt not commit adultery," and its exposition by Christ that "lust is tantamount to adultery," have to say to modern Christians about their television and movie viewing habits? How does the commandment to tithe from the first fruits work in an economy where income is taxed, and where a certain portion of income is taken and theoretically "set aside" for future income? How do Paul's admonitions to submit to the ruling authorities, which are ordained of God, function in a modern democratic state where the governors rule by consent of the governed? Many more questions could be asked, and yet these examples show how the timeless principles of the Scriptures must be brought to bear on contemporary life, even if it is often difficult to understand how. As an interpreter and expositor of God's Word, it is your high calling and privilege to show people how to do so.

As in the task of interpretation, there are helpful principles one brings to bear on the task of application. The first principle is to ask questions of the text. What is the primary emphasis of this text? Is it calling upon me primarily to know a fact, believe a truth, or obey a command? Then, when I have determined which of those is the primary emphasis (and more than one element may be involved), how am I to respond? What implications does this text have for my life—the way I think about the world around me—and what I will or will not do? How does this text call upon me to change my thought, beliefs or ethics? Again, all of these will be expounded as the individual chapters take up the particular portions of the Scripture.

Do You Understand What You Are Reading?

One cardinal rule in making good applications is to distinguish carefully between what is a proverb (or pious advice) and what is a law. The Scriptures contain laws—those things by which we are to govern our lives. They also contain advice, which is a more fluid category. For instance, in 1 Corinthians 7:8, Paul says that it is good for those who are unmarried to remain single. He then explains the reasons for that advice, but acknowledges that it is not desirable for many people. It is not a command; it is advice. This is true of the book of Proverbs, too, where we are told, in Proverbs 26:4 (NAS), "Do not answer a fool according to his folly," and then in the immediately following verse we are told to "Answer a fool as his folly deserves." Clearly, there are situations when it is wiser not to answer a fool, and situations where it is wiser to answer him appropriately.

Likewise, we must not confuse proverbs with promises. There are general rules of life given to us in Proverbs. Proverbs 28:16 states that honest rulers will enjoy long reigns. Yet, Josiah of Judah was a just ruler, and was killed in battle. Clearly, Solomon is giving a wise principle—those who govern well are more likely to survive longer than those who invoke the hatred of those under them. The same could be said for Proverbs 22:6, "Train up a child in the way he should go; even when he is old he will not depart from it." This is a proverb, not a promise. Clearly, Solomon is right. Patterns of ethics and behavior taught in childhood tend to be firmly rooted in the adult life. But, this is not a promise that those who raise their children in accordance with God's word are inevitably guaranteed they will become believers. One only needs to think of the difference between Cain and Abel, or Jacob and Esau, to see the fallacy of that line of thinking. Proverbs are guides for a wise life; promises are unconditional guarantees of God to bless his children.

There is one final principle to keep in mind here, and that is simply this: when it comes to making accurate applications of the teachings of the Scripture, *historical or descriptive passages are to be interpreted by didactic or teaching passages of Scripture*. Many interpreters have failed at precisely this point. Bible teachers have concluded that, because Rahab lied to save the Israelite spies in Jericho, and was rewarded, that it is permissible to lie in situations when a person does not deserve the truth. We would do better to follow Anselm who rightly said, "If God were to tell a lie, it would not therefore follow that it is right to lie, but that God is not God." We have the clear and unstipulated commandment of God that we are not to bear false witness. It is the commandment, and not the historical example, that is to govern our behavior. The historical portions of the Scripture can show us, by example, great truths that are taught to us elsewhere. Yet, we must be careful never to derive a doctrine or an ethic merely from historical portions of Scripture.

Clearly, there is much here to digest. The truths here expounded will be unfolded in subsequent chapters. So, on with learning how to know and apply God's Word—it is the highest and most holy task anyone can aspire to do. And, if we have been faithful, those who profit from our teaching will sing Christian's song upon leaving the Interpreter's house:

Here I have seen things rare and profitable,
Things pleasant, dreadful, things to make me stable
In what I have begun to take in hand;
Then let me think on them, and understand
Wherefore they shewed me were, and let me be
Thankful, O good Interpreter, to thee.

Chapter Three
God's Story: Historical Narrative

Everybody likes a good story. The success of Barnes and Noble or Waldenbooks is proof of that. It was that way long before the invention of the printing press, or even of scrolls. The storyteller was important, not only as an entertainer, but as a teacher and philosopher long before the ability to read and write was widely possessed. He has been largely displaced in modern times by the author and the publisher. Now a few dollars will buy a good romance or adventure or mystery novel, but that has only enabled the art form to reach the general public to an extent unheard of in earlier times.

But who is the greatest storyteller of all? Who thought up the grandest, most complete, most interlocking yet most consistent plot of all stories? You know the answer, of course. This greatest storyteller of all is God, and the story is the Bible. And, most importantly to us, this story is absolutely true. God has not only conceived the plot, but He has created the world and all that is in it in accordance with this plan, and He has worked out all of this in history. Then, through the human writers whom He inspired, He has recorded for us this account of the outworking of his plan.

This story is told on two levels. The "upper level" is a grand description of the way God has worked in history, and continues to work, to accomplish his purposes. In this story, we find the epic sweep of God's mighty acts, all working together to his glory. It is a panoramic view of the creation and the fall, the establishment of a people of faith through Abraham, a nation peculiar to Himself through Israel. All of this leads to the climactic gift of the Redeemer, God's own Son, Jesus, the Christ, who has redeemed his people and established his kingdom even in this fallen earth. In the New Testament narrative of Acts, we see the amazing growth of that kingdom. But the last chapter is not narrated—it is prophesied and it is taught in epistles and apocalypse. That day will come when this world will be destroyed, along with the forces of darkness, and the myriads of the redeemed ones will gather at the heavenly throne to praise the triune God.

The second level consists of the multitude of individual incidents into which the grand account is broken. These are the "Bible stories" which we like to read and to teach to our children. Our hard work of biblical interpretation has to be done on this level. Whether it is the story of Gideon and the fleece or of David and Goliath, this is where we have to deal with the words and sentences and paragraphs that make up the story. This is where we have to determine what the Bible really says, and then determine how it might apply to us today. This is where we are going to concentrate our attention in this chapter. Yet we should never lose sight of the "upper level" overview and we should be aware of how any individual story fits into the grand scheme.

Perhaps some of you have read some of *Aesop's* Fables. One of the best known of these is "The Hare and the Tortoise," in which the hare challenged the tortoise to a race. After he was far, far ahead of the tortoise, the hare laid down and took a nap. Several hours later, he awoke to see the tortoise crossing the finish line. The story ends with the moral: "Plodding wins the race." Of course, this is a made-up story, while the Bible is truth, but the important point for our consideration here is that the story taught a lesson, and that it ended with an explicit statement of that lesson. This is rarely the case with Biblical narration.

Some of us have read as children, or have read to our children, a good children's Bible storybook. The book tells the story of some passage of Scripture in language a child can easily understand. Often the story ends with a moral lesson that the passage illustrates. This lesson is usually correct and appropriate, but it was not found in the biblical account itself. For example, one excellent book of this type tells the story of the bronze serpent in the wilderness, saying that, if anyone had been bitten by a serpent, he could look up at the brass serpent and he would get well. It concludes, "In the same way, any sinner may find salvation by lifting up his eyes [in faith] and looking at Christ on the cross." That is fine for teaching children (or even adults), but it is not in the Old Testament passage being taught. We would not find this lesson in Numbers 21; it is imported from John 3:14-15.

One thing that is almost universally true of the narrative, or storytelling, passages of Scripture is that the account of the facts of the incident is given plainly, with no explicit lesson presented to the reader. The immediate purpose of the narrative passage is to record what happened. It is only rarely that an explicit lesson or message is tied to the account. It follows that we should be careful not to read into the passage a message that it does not contain.

For example, consider the story of Jacob obtaining the blessing from Isaac, as told in Genesis 27. Jacob, on the advice of his mother, dealt falsely with his father, Isaac, by pretending to be his brother, Esau. Through Jacob's deception, Isaac gave him the blessing he intended for Esau. There are many lessons we might be tempted to find in this passage. (1) A grown man should not follow his mother's advice. (2) A lie is all right if the purpose is good. (3) God caused Jacob to lie in order to carry out his purpose. (4) A man should prepare a will long before he grows old and feeble. (5) God can use the results of sin to his own glory. (6) God forgives the sins of those who turn to Him. Some of these lessons are true, but some are abominable. The point is that none of these lessons are found in the text of the passage. They are all superimposed upon the story.

How, then, should we go about interpreting the passage? First, we should read it. Then read it again, preferably in a different translation. Read the previous chapter and the following one, to be sure of the context. Then read it in detail to see exactly what each sentence is saying. Keep the cultural context in mind—that this was in the Patriarchal Age, and the leadership of the clan was handed down from father to son. From this, we can see the importance of this blessing. In fact, we can learn from this story, a little more about that culture, since the blessing, once given, could not be changed. Keeping the "upper level" story also in mind, we can see that this was a critical point in God's working out his purpose among his people. Our reading of the text back in Genesis 25 shows us that all of this was in the foreordination of God, who had told Isaac (through Rebekah) that the older would serve the younger. Our reading forward into Chapter 28 shows us that Isaac, once the blessing was given, did not resent Jacob, but continued to bless him.

But in all of this, we do not find a lesson spelled out which we can apply to our own day and situation. We cannot say, "See, this teaches us that ..." We can go to other passages, for instance Lev. 19:11 (KJV) and read, "Ye shall not steal, neither deal falsely, neither lie one to another." Then, observing how Jacob was cheated by his great uncle Laban, we can conclude that God does, indeed, chasten his own. However, the passage under consideration does not teach this lesson in itself. Rather, it illustrates a lesson taught elsewhere.

There is another thing to remember in an account such as this. This incident is but one scene of a much larger narrative of the life of Jacob, which, in turn, is but one act in the "upper level" story of God's mighty works. We can easily miss the significance of portions of this story if we are not familiar with the larger story of Jacob's life, as in our reference above to Chapters 25 and 28. Not only that, but the facts of this incident contribute greatly to our appreciation of the larger story. We can see why he was named "Jacob," or "Supplanter," and we can see the marvelous grace of God in renaming him "Israel," or "Prince of God," after his conversion.

One other caution is appropriate. Be careful in applying Bible stories to yourself in your present situation. Our cultural context is greatly different

God's Story: Historical Narrative

from that of Bible times. Our specific options are different. It is one thing to read of Abraham and ask ourselves, "Could I possibly have the kind of faith that he showed?" That could help motivate us to grow in faith. It is quite another to say, "This is what Abraham did, so I should do that also." After all, Abraham offered his wife to Pharaoh and to Abimelech. Or consider the account of Gideon in Judges 6-8. Gideon was a mighty man of valor.— eventually. But how many people read the story and become convinced that they should put out figurative fleeces to determine God's will for themselves? They overlook the fact that the placing of the fleece was a sign of an initially weak courage and faith, to which God graciously condescended.

All of this can be summed up by a principle given by R. C. Sproul: historical narratives must be interpreted by the didactic[1]. That is, those passages that tell us what happened do not teach us ethics or doctrine. There are passages which are given for the purpose of teaching these things.

In the narrative passages, we often encounter descriptions of miraculous happenings. Although it should go without saying, it is important enough to be stressed anyway: accept these accounts as truth, just as they are written. God is the God of

---

[1] Knowing Scripture, R. C. Sproul, InterVarsity Press, Downers Grove, IL, 1977

truth. All of his word is truth. He is powerful enough to work miracles. Nothing within his will is impossible to Him. After all, He was able to create the universe in six days.

The Bible consists of more narrative passages than of any other type. Genesis, much of Exodus and Numbers, and all the books from Joshua through Esther are primarily narrative. In addition, many of the prophetic books contain much narrative material. And that's just the Old Testament. In the New Testament, much of the Gospel accounts, together with Acts, also are narrative.

The narrative portions of the Gospels are so distinctive that a separate chapter will be devoted to them, together with the parables. But it would be wise to give special attention also to the Book of Acts, which consists mostly of narrative material, together with some teaching and prophetic material. For the most part, the teaching and prophetic material are embedded in the narrative.

Acts presents a particular challenge to the interpreter. The fact that it describes the church in the early days of the New Covenant heightens the temptation to misinterpret passages that "tell it like it was" as passages that "tell it like it should be." It is very easy to read of a certain incident in this book and assume that it shows a pattern which should be observed in the church today. Many teachers seem to have as their ideal a return to the "New Testament Church" as described in Acts.

Such a return is impossible. Caesar and the Sanhedrin are not around to persecute us. The Apostles are not around to teach us. But, even if it were possible, it would not be desirable. For example, the tremendous changes in communications technology since that time give us great opportunities in missions and evangelism, which we would be foolish to ignore.

In the account Luke has given us in the Book of Acts, we find tremendous examples of love for the brethren, of courage, of self-sacrifice and of diligence. But Luke never once stops to say, "Go and do thou likewise." For that, we must turn to the Gospels or the Epistles, where all of these qualities are taught. In 1 Corinthians 13, Paul teaches us what love for one another is. Over and over, in the Book of Acts, we can see that love in action. If Paul's teaching didn't get beyond our minds to our hearts, Luke's examples should do just that.

We must not assume that a particular action or pattern in the early church requires that we follow that pattern. For example, Acts 3:44-45 and 5:32-36 tell us that in the very early Jerusalem church, the believers sold their possessions and pooled their resources. This was a good example of love for one another in action. Does this mean that we should now live in some sort of theocratic communism? There have been some modern communal movements seeking to follow this pattern. Yet a careful study of both Acts and the Epistles will show that such a pattern was not typical of other churches, and certainly was not followed at Antioch (Acts 11:29), although the principle of giving freely continued to be followed.

There is a remarkable mutually reinforcing relationship between the narrative books, such as Acts, and the teaching books, such as the Epistles. The narrative books tell us what has happened. They do not usually tell us explicitly whether that happening was good or bad, whether it was wise or foolish. For that, we must go to the teaching passages to learn the truths which can be applied to the history. Only in that way can we fully appreciate how any incident fits into the "upper level" story. At the same time, the teaching passages speak the truth to us primarily through our minds and understanding. While the understanding of the truth can reach our hearts to affect our lives, it is through the narrative passages that this connection is most effectively made. When Paul said (2 Tim. 4:2 NAS), "Preach the word...reprove, rebuke, exhort with great patience and instruction," a young pastor understands his responsibility. When he sees how Peter and Paul lived this principle out in their lives, he knows in his heart as well as his mind what his calling is, and he is much better prepared to fill that calling well. Laymen can read that passage and rationalize, "That is great for *the preacher*," but when they turn to Acts 8, they find that it was everyone *but* the Apostles who were scattered and went everywhere "preaching the word."

Of course, there are passages in this book that are specifically devoted to teaching. For example, the sermons of Peter and of Paul, as well as the defenses of Peter, Stephen and Paul, have much teaching content. The Jerusalem Council of Acts 15 was called specifically to deal with the doctrinal matter of the requirements to be placed upon the Gentile believers. Passages such as these are important, and can be used profitably, to help us to refine our understanding of both doctrine and practice in a biblically faithful way.

In light of what has been said above, it is fair to ask, "What is important about the Book of Acts?" The answer to this is four-fold. First, there is what appears to be Luke's own purpose in writing the book. He has given us a broad, but often detailed, account of the growth of the church, from a band of about 120 disciples (1:15), to many thousands in Jerusalem, to Antioch, Asia, Greece, and Rome itself, with many points in between. It is an amazing testimony to the power of the Holy Spirit working in and through those who follow Jesus.

Second, the book is filled with illustrations of the application of principles taught elsewhere. Third, in the descriptions of the experiences of the disciples, we can learn much about the culture of the various places at that time, assisting us in the study of other books. Finally, there are those teaching passages, such as mentioned above, which give us specific instruction in the faith.

Chapter Four
"Why the Law, Then?"

Of what use is the moral law to all men?

The moral law is of use to all men, to inform them of the holy nature and will of God, and of their duty, binding them to walk accordingly; to convince them of their disability to keep it, and of the sinful pollution of their nature, hearts, and lives: to humble them in the sense of their sin and misery, and thereby help them to a clearer sight of the need they have of Christ, and of the perfection of his obedience.

-The Westminster Larger Catechism Q. 95

The whole question of the Law is one of great controversy in evangelical circles. Some teach that the Law of God does nothing but point the unbeliever to Christ, and has no continuing real function in the life of the individual believer, or society at large. Their chorus could well be, "Free from the Law, O happy condition! Jesus hath bled, and there is remission."

On the other end of the continuum, Theonomic Reconstructionists believe that the whole of the moral and civil Law of the Old Testament, in exhaustive detail, is applicable both to the believer and to society at large. Thus, if the Old Testament civil code calls upon us to stone rebellious children, that is what we must do.

The Reformed, or covenantal, hermeneutic strikes a balance between these two positions. It heartily agrees with Lutherans and other evangelicals in asserting that the Law cannot save. Romans 3:20, 28 says, "For by works of the law no human being will be justified in his sight, since through the law comes knowledge of sin...For we hold that one is justified by faith apart from works of the law." In this respect, the Law is the schoolmaster that leads us to Christ (Galatians 3:24). It is, as Luther was fond of saying, "the hammer of God that smashes our own self-righteousness, and the mirror of God that shows us our own sinfulness."

But, that is not all that the Law was designed to do. It has a continuing function, both in the life of the believer, and in the ordering of the affairs of men and nations. Matthew 5:18 quotes Jesus, "For truly, I say to you, until heaven and earth pass away, not an iota, not a dot, will pass from the Law until all is accomplished." And, Paul says that the Law is holy, righteous and good (Romans 7:12); and that the regenerate man delights in the law of God in his inner being (Romans 7:22). He then answers a possible misunderstanding of his own teaching, Romans 3:31, "Do we then overthrow the law by this faith? By no means! On the contrary, we uphold the law."

If we are to do justice to these verses, we must state that there is at least one sense in which the Law has been abolished, and another sense in which it has not. But, how is the interpreter to make sense of this? Fortunately, the *Westminster Confession of Faith* is of great help in this regard. It will help us to interpret and apply the Law of God in this day of grace.

But, before we begin, we must be clear at what we mean by the Law of God. Broadly construed, the Law is the first five books of the Old Testament, authored by Moses, sometimes called the *Pentateuch* or the *Torah*. It must be admitted from the first, that there is much more material in these books than Law. There is much narrative—the stories of the creation, the flood, the patriarchal history, and the Exodus. Principles for interpreting those portions can be found in our previous chapter.

Our concern is with the Law proper, as it begins in Exodus 20, and includes the complete books of Leviticus and Deuteronomy, then concludes in Numbers 19. It is an important concern because the Law is a neglected topic among preachers and teachers in our day. Unlike our Puritan forebears, we don't know how to handle and apply it rightly.

We must remember Paul's counsel to Timothy in 1 Timothy 1:8, "Now we know that the law is good, if one uses it lawfully". Right preaching of the Law brings conviction of sin, faith in the Savior, and fruitfulness to the Christian life. This chapter, I hope, will serve somewhat as a revival of teaching the Law in the light of the eternal covenant of grace, and the blessed Gospel of Christ.

As we stated in Chapter Two, the covenant forms the basis for understanding and applying the Scriptures. The whole Bible is a covenantal document, and the Scriptures, read from Genesis to Revelation, show us the unfolding of God's covenant of grace in human history.

But, what does that mean, and how does it govern interpretation? When God enters into relationship with human beings, individually or corporately, he always does so by means of a covenant. This has been defined various ways, but in essence, a covenant is encapsulated in God's statement to Israel, "I will be your God, and you will be my people." A covenant is God's voluntary condescension to man, in which God legally binds himself to his people, and by which they are bound to him. In certain respects, a covenant is like a contract, but it must be remembered that we do not enter into this legal bond as equal partners. God sets the terms of the relationship, and those terms are non-negotiable. In every covenant, there are great blessings attached to fulfillment of the terms, and curses for disobedience to its terms. But, what makes the covenant of grace a magnanimous arrangement is that God, in Christ, has arranged for the fulfillment of his own terms, and through him has borne the penalties for our disobedience himself! In short, Christ fulfills the obedience God's covenant requires, and bears the penalties of our disobedience, so that we receive only the blessings of the covenant—and we receive them by faith alone.

We must note that the Scripture teaches one covenant of grace, not many covenants of grace. The successive post-fall covenants are those made with and through Noah, Abraham, Moses, and David. Each of those covenants is a successive administration of the one covenant of grace— man's right standing with God is always by grace through faith. We notice similar features in all of them. In each, there is a great promise of God to bless his people, and a requirement that his people obey him. Each one of them is made with one man, a mediator, but through that one man, to result in a blessing to many. As God said to Abraham, "in you shall all the nations of the earth be blessed."

Of the most significance is that all of these covenants find the fulfillment of their stipulations and promises *in Christ*. Therefore, those that are in Christ are the recipients of all the promises of the covenants, freely, by the grace of God. Christ has fulfilled all the obligations of these covenants, and he has met all the penalties; he has handed the promises to us on far better terms.

Understanding the covenantal nature of the Law will help us understand three key foundational principles for interpreting and applying the Law. First, the promise (Christ pays the penalty of sin) does not annul the Law, but was added because of sin. Second, the Law can never make the sinner righteous. This is not a defect in the Law, which remains "holy, just, and good," but the defect is in the sinner who cannot keep the law. Third, when a person receives a new heart and a new nature through the promise, his relationship to the Law changes. It no longer solely speaks sin and death to him, but also serves as a guide for the holy life.

In Galatians 3:17-26, the Apostle Paul teaches us how the Christian ought to view the Law:

> [17]This is what I mean: the law, which came 430 years afterward, does not annul a covenant previously ratified by God, so as to make the promise void. [18]For if the inheritance comes by the law, it no longer comes by promise; but God gave it to Abraham by a promise. [19]Why then the law? It was added because of transgressions, until the offspring should come to whom the

"Why the Law, Then?"

promise had been made, and it was put in place through angels by an intermediary. ... ²¹Is the law then contrary to the promises of God? Certainly not! For if a law had been given that could give life, then righteousness would indeed be by the law. ²²But the Scripture imprisoned everything under sin, so that the promise by faith in Jesus Christ might be given to those who believe. ²³Now before faith came, we were held captive under the law, imprisoned until the coming faith would be revealed. ²⁴So then, the law was our guardian until Christ came, in order that we might be justified by faith. ²⁵But now that faith has come, we are no longer under a guardian, ²⁶for in Christ Jesus you are all sons of God, through faith.

The first point Paul makes about the Law is that it does not set aside the covenant of grace, but is rather superadded to it. In other words, salvation is by grace through faith. That is God's promise. The Law did not come along and make salvation dependent upon obedience. "Why then the Law?"

In the first place, the Law was given to show us what sin was (Romans 7:7), and thus drive us to Christ. The Law holds the unbeliever captive—he is confronted with his own inability to keep it (Romans 2:15). As the *Larger Catechism* says, "The moral law is of use to unregenerate men, to awaken their consciences to flee from wrath to come, and to drive them to Christ; or, upon their continuance in the estate and way of sin, to leave them inexcusable, and under the curse thereof."

But, the Law is not an end in itself, and it could never save a sinner. The reason why is quite simple: if you break one of the laws, you are guilty of breaking the whole Law (James 2:10). And, what is more, subsequent acts of obedience would simply be to render to God what is his due—they could never make up for past disobedience.

One might think of it this way: a bank employee, over a course of years, embezzles $100,000. He stands before a jury of his peers, caught red-handed. His plea is this, "I did it, but I promise not to do it in the future. And, what is more, I will stop lying, too." Does that make up for his past crimes? No. If he is truly to atone for his crime, he must repay the debt. One cannot atone for his sins by simply resolving to obey henceforth. Payment must be made. The payment for disobedience demanded by God's covenant sanction is death.

Thus, the Law brings only condemnation to the unbeliever. It places him under the sentence of death, and helps him realize there is nothing he can do, in and of himself, to escape that curse. In short, it readies him for the Gospel. The wonderful truth of the Gospel is that it promises life to those who were dead in sin, through faith in Christ, apart from the works of the Law. As Paul writes in Ephesians 2:1-5:

> [1]And you were dead in the trespasses and sins [2]in which you once walked, following the course of this world, following the prince of the power of the air, the spirit that is now at work in the sons of disobedience—[3]among whom we all once lived in the passions of our flesh, carrying out the desires of the body and the mind, and were by nature children of wrath, like the rest of mankind. [4]But God, being rich in mercy, because of the great love with which he loved us, [5]even when we were dead in our trespasses, made us alive together with Christ—by grace you have been saved—

And when that new life begins, the believer discovers that very instrument of oppression to his guilty conscience becomes for him a blessed guide, not for earning a salvation already freely obtained by grace, but rather in living out the new life in covenant with God.

As a covenantal document, the Law has traditionally been divided into three parts: moral, civil and ceremonial law. These parts are not distinct, but interrelated. The moral law serves as the basis of the whole Law. It is most clearly expressed in the Ten Commandments (Exodus 20; Deuteronomy 5). The civil law was the application of the moral law to the particular culture and historical situation of Israel. The ceremonial law displayed God's provision of forgiveness for those who broke the Law, through sacrifice (ultimately, Christ's sacrifice). Also, its provisions of food and cleanliness regulations proclaimed that Israel was to be distinct from the nations in all that she did, even the most mundane facets of her daily life: her food and her clothing.

Perhaps the best explanation of this can be found in *The Westminster Confession of Faith*, chapter 19, as well as the exposition of the Law given in *The Westminster Larger Catechism*, Q.91 through Q.152. The moral law contains the eternal precepts of God—what is always right and always wrong in all ages and situations. It "doth forever bind all, as well justified persons as others, to the obedience thereof." (*WCF* 19.5).

The ceremonial law, as Hebrews teaches us, "prefigur[es] Christ, his graces, actions, sufferings and benefits." (*WCF* 19.3). It has been abrogated—that is, these laws no longer bind, because they foreshadowed Christ, and he has fulfilled them.

The civil law, the application of the moral law to the life of God's people under the Old Covenant (the covenant of law), has "expired together with the state of that people, not obliging any other now, further than the general equity thereof may require." (*WCF* 19.4) In short, the civil law was the moral law applied to a particular nation, time and place.

The civil law provides principles showing *how* the Law can be applied to a society (general equity), but in its particulars, it has ceased to apply. In the modern industrial and technological world, the concern may not be goring another's ox (though it may be in agrarian societies), but it may be infringement of patent and copyright. The civil law shows us how a society ordered on godly principles might address such things.

While the principles never change, the applications of such principles must change as society changes. Principles like restitution for losses caused by criminal conduct and leaving fields with ample food for gleaning could be implemented in modern society, thus making it both more just and merciful, as a reflection of God's holy character, and his will for all humanity, though the particulars of the application may change from society to society.

It is important to emphasize that the abrogation and cessation of the ceremonial and civil law does not mean we are to skip these portions of Scripture in our teaching. Rather, it governs how they are to be taught. If the lesson before us is from the ceremonial law, and governs, for example, the regulations of temple worship, one would study: (1) what the regulations were, (2) what they meant for Israel, and (3) how they prefigure Christ and the New Covenant.

Now, it must be noted that, while the principles are straightforward, it does not therefore follow that it will be immediately apparent either what the symbolism was for Israel, or how every text specifically points to Christ. This is where it is necessary to have compiled reliable helps such as the commentaries or study Bibles mentioned in the earlier chapter. Cross-references are very helpful in this regard.

The ceremonial cleanliness regulations and food laws present their own unique challenges, but ought not to be neglected. All Scripture is God-breathed, and therefore profitable! It is easier to understand and apply these laws if we understand the supremacy of holiness in the lives of those who serve God. The principle:

> "For I am the Lord who brought you up out of the land of Egypt to be your God. You shall therefore be holy, for I am holy" (Leviticus 11:45)

is repeated again and again throughout the ceremonial law. It is the chief governing principle. It is not difficult, then, to draw application even from laws that no longer apply. God's demand of holiness invaded the life of the average Israelite at every turn. It was not just for the temple, but regulated what he ate and what he wore. It reached into his clothes closet, his refrigerator and his marriage bed. Now, while the manifestation of that high call to holiness has changed, the principle has not. Abraham Kuyper said long ago, "There is not one square inch of life over which Christ, who is Lord of all, has not laid the claim 'It is mine.'" Just as Israel was, we are to be holy in all we do. There is nothing that escapes God's notice, or that is exempted from his Lordship. Paul reminds us, "So, whether you eat or drink, or whatever you do, do all to the glory of God." (1 Corinthians 10:31)

The ceremonial law has been the victim of rampant speculation over the years. Even well respected biblical scholars have been less than chaste in their treatment of the ceremonial law. Some have speculated God gave the kosher law primarily for health reasons. The text does not tell us this, and, one must wonder, if the kosher provisions primarily concerned health, why are they no longer in effect for Christians? Therefore, be especially cautious not to speculate what the reason or symbolism might have been behind commands, if the reason is not readily apparent from the text. I once heard a well-known television preacher speculate that the prohibition given to

Israel against eating animals with cloven hoofs meant that Christians must completely separate themselves from unbelievers. I wonder what the man did with 1 Corinthians 5:10, where believers are commanded *not* to separate themselves from unbelievers. Those types of application have no root in the text whatsoever.

The moral law, as the crown and fountainhead of all divine law, is the easiest to expound and apply. Jesus taught us much about the right use of the Law in how he interpreted and applied it. The first principle that Jesus shows us is that the Law is not narrow, but broad in its application. Matthew 5:21-22, 27-28:

> ^{21}You have heard that it was said to those of old, "You shall not murder; and whoever murders will be liable to judgment." ^{22}But I say to you that everyone who is angry with his brother will be liable to judgment; whoever insults his brother will be liable to the council; and whoever says, "You fool!" will be liable to the hell of fire. ^{27}You have heard that it was said, "You shall not commit adultery." ^{28}But I say to you that everyone who looks at a woman with lustful intent has already committed adultery with her in his heart.

Jesus did this on numerous occasions, chastising the Pharisees for their alternately

"Why the Law, Then?"

narrow and picayunish understanding of the Law. At root, the Pharisees' problem (sometimes called "legalism") is not that they were too assiduous or diligent in their obedience to God, but rather that they elevated obedience to their manmade rules with heartfelt obedience to God, and that their justice was not tempered by mercy. And, as man inevitably does when he undertakes to write divine law himself, the Pharisees left massive loopholes that eviscerated the merciful heart of God's intention in the Law—in short, they "strained at gnats and swallowed camels."

We must be careful in our application of the principles of the Law to the situations that modern Christians face, that we do not begin to legislate behaviors. Rather, we are to give principles and examples, and help people to think through the ramifications of the law for their own circumstances.

For instance, it is a basic Reformed hermeneutical principle that whatever command is not specifically repealed in the New Testament continues in effect. The Sabbath command, a gift of God, made for man, continues to serve as God's gracious provision. Therefore, it is important that we teach that God built man to work six days and to rest and worship on one. We need to help people see how this ought to affect their behaviors. How does God's mandated rest for "manservants and maidservants" speak to our modern penchant for convenient dining and shopping on the Lord's Day? Is it not the duty of Christian employers to allow their employees to rest on the Lord's Day?

Admittedly, there is a fine line here between helping people to apply principles to their own situation and to think through obeying the spirit of the Law on the one side, or mandating manmade "thou shalt not's" on the other. The principle is clear: one day for rest and worship, not just for ourselves, but for those in our employ.

If we understand the Law in all its depth and richness, grasp how it functions in the life of the unbeliever and the believer, see how it serves the Gospel, and enjoy its blessings as a child of God, the Lord will bless those who learn from us how to lead a productive, God-ward, and joyful Christian life.

Chapter Five
Lovelier Than Trees: Poetry in the Scriptures

"I think that I shall never see a poem lovely as a tree." *Sgt. Joyce Kilmer*

"Blessed is the man who walks not in the counsel of the wicked, nor stands in the way of sinners, nor sits in the seat of scoffers; but his delight is in the law of the LORD, and on his law he meditates day and night. He is like a tree planted by streams of water that yields its fruit in its season, and its leaf does not wither. In all that he does, he prospers." (Psalm 1:1-3)

Modern Americans do not have much use for poetry. Many have less than fond memories of memorizing Shakespeare sonnets, or poems by Tennyson and Donne in high school. It strikes our ears as artificial, flowery and foreign. Yet, in the ancient world, where both literacy and printed matter were scarce, poetry and ode were prized as ways of communicating vast amounts of material in a memorable format, just as it is far easier for us to remember the words of a much-loved hymn, or a catchy commercial jingle than the prose of even a beloved novel.

The poetic books of the Bible, Psalms and Song of Solomon, contain a wealth of beautiful, meaningful and familiar refrains about God and his world. We turn to the Psalms in times of trouble, looking for comfort in the familiar refrains of the Psalm 23, Psalm 46, or Psalm 90. When we feel laden with sin, and in need of forgiveness and grace, we look to Psalm 32, or Psalm 51. We use Psalm 103 to give voice to our gratitude in times of blessing. We see the footprints of the Lord Jesus, "great David's greater son" in the royal and Messianic Psalms such as Psalm 2, Psalm 72, or Psalm 110. The Psalms were the songbook of Israel, and, because of that fact, the sole songbook of the infant Reformed churches.

Yet, despite their familiarity to us, the poetry of the Psalms often falls strangely upon the modern ear. English poetry leads us to expect devices like rhyme and meter that, while not lacking from Hebrew poetry, certainly do not often come through in translations. And, were one to undertake to explain the beauty, cleverness or genius of the original poetry, he would certainly trample the very thing that makes the Psalm beautiful or moving in the first place. Sometimes, we can trample the beauty of a thing by over-analysis, and we must be careful not to do that when it comes to biblical poetry. The analysis should inform our study and presentation, but not be allowed to subvert the intention of the Author, who chose to communicate truth in the medium of beautiful poetry.

But, that is not the sole consideration that makes teaching or preaching biblical poetry difficult. Many of the Psalms are given to us bereft of their historical setting. So, while we can look to context to help us understand a parable of Jesus, or the argument of one of Paul's letters, very often we are left on our own when it comes to a Psalm.

All of this being said, it is important to remember that the Psalms are precious Holy Scripture, and ought to be familiar to God's people, memorized, preached and taught. As mentioned earlier, the Psalms are songs. Thus, the chief intention of the Psalms is always to inform and shape the praise of God's people for his glorious character and his wondrous acts to the children of men. This must be kept in mind at all times when studying the Psalms. They are God's own inspired praise, intended by him to be used by us so that we might praise him rightly. For a fuller, yet concise and accessible, treatment, you may want to purchase Tremper Longman, III's, book *How to Read the Psalms* (Downers Grove, IL: IVP, 1988)

The poetic passages of the Scriptures are certainly not limited to Psalms and Song of Solomon, but are also found in the songs of Hannah, Deborah, Miriam, Solomon, and in the writings of Paul. The principles laid down there can certainly be judiciously applied to other biblical poetry and songs as well.

The structure of poetry helps us understand its meaning. Gordon Fee and Douglas Stuart, in their book, *How to Read the Bible for All Its Worth*, make the helpful point that a good starting point for understanding Hebrew poetry is by using a Bible dictionary, and simply looking under the heading "poetry" or "Hebrew poetry." They stress the importance of understanding three functions of the repetitive style of Old Testament poetry:

1) Synonymous parallelism. The second or subsequent line repeats or reinforces the sense of the first line:

    The heavens declare the glory of God, and the sky above proclaims his handiwork. Day to day pours out speech, and night to night reveals knowledge. (Psalm 19:1-2)

Understanding synonymous parallelism means that we understand the Psalmist is not trying to say four separate things about God's revelation of himself in the created world, but rather two things (the skies declare God's glory and power, and they do it without ceasing). (Fee & Stuart, p. 171).

2) Antithetical parallelism. The second or subsequent line contrasts the thought of the first:

> They do not cry to me from the heart, but they wail upon their beds; for grain and wine they gash themselves; they rebel against me. (Hosea 7:14)

3) Synthetic parallelism. The second or subsequent line adds to the first line in a manner that provides further information (Fee & Stuart, p. 162):

> Saviors shall go up to Mount Zion to rule Mount Esau, and the kingdom shall be the LORD's. (Obadiah 1:21)

Psalms are poetic representations of the truth. It is important to remember that, because the Psalms are poetic songs, the concern of the Holy Spirit in inspiring them is not to make explicit doctrinal statements, but to express the truth in poetic imagery, allusion, metaphor, and simile. God is not really a fortress, but rather is *like* a fortress in that he protects his people from trouble. When the authors use metaphors, it is important to find the truth they are expressing in the metaphor.

Types of Psalms. There are different genres of literature within the Psalter itself. Fee and Stuart give the following principles:

1) The psalms are characterized by types (listed below). Knowing these types helps interpret the meaning of each psalm.

2) Each psalm is characterized by its form or structure that it shares with other psalms. Knowing the structure of a psalm helps to understand what is happening within it. Transition from subject to subject, repetition of ideas, etc., help uncover the central concern of the psalmist.

3) The patterns of speech in psalms give us cues as to their central messages.

4) Each Psalm is a self-contained literary unit. Unlike the Gospels, where each paragraph ought to be read in light of the context, and of the whole book, each Psalm was written independently, and then compiled into a collection, and thus each stands alone. (Fee & Stuart, p. 172-173).

These are arbitrary categories, to be sure, but aid us in understanding the meaning of each psalm. Tremper Longman notes the following forms (with an example):

1) The hymn (Psalm 103). Hymns begin with a call to worship, continue by expanding the reasons for God's praiseworthiness, and,

often conclude with further ascriptions of praise (Longman, p. 24).

2) The lament (Psalm 22). The lament expresses the depths of relationship with God in times of sorrow, the feelings of abandonment and distress, and pleas to God to help. (Longman, p. 27-29) The pattern of laments is as follows:

    a) Address
    b) Complaint
    c) Trust
    d) Deliverance
    e) Assurance
    f) Praise (Fee & Stuart, p. 178)

3) Psalms of thanksgiving (Psalm 56). A thanksgiving psalm is a hymn of praise to God for rescuing his people from a particular difficulty. (Longman, p. 30) The pattern of thanksgiving psalms is:

    a) A Summary of the situation
    b) The distressing circumstance
    c) Plea for help
    d) How God answered the plea
    e) Testimony to God's mercy

4) Psalms of confidence (Psalm 46). [These] express trust in God's goodness and power. They are grouped by tone and content, rather than structure. The psalmist asserts his trust

in God despite his present circumstances. (Longman, p. 31)

5) Psalms of remembrance (Psalm 77). These recall God's covenant faithfulness as it is demonstrated in the history of God's people, often in the Exodus, or in the establishment of the Davidic royal line (Longman, p. 32)

6) Wisdom Psalms (Psalm 119). Wisdom psalms teach the great benefits that come from ordering one's life in accordance with God's word. (Longman, p. 32-33)

7) Kingship (or Messianic) Psalms (Psalm 72) extol God's faithfulness in raising up a king, and point us to "great David's greater Son," the last, greatest, and coming king of God's spiritual Israel. (Longman, p. 34-35)

How to Interpret a Psalm: A Brief. By now, one can sense the difficulty that comes in interpreting the Psalms. Here, especially, a good study Bible or a brief commentary, such as one mentioned in the introductory chapter, is most useful. The more you study the Psalms with tools, the more you will see the structure that is at work in each psalm, and the more, then, each psalm will speak to you. To give you an idea of how to analyze a psalm, here is an example of analysis:

Lovelier Than Trees: Poetry in the Scriptures

Psalm 2:1-12

¹Why do the nations rage and the peoples plot in vain?

²The kings of the earth set themselves, and the rulers take counsel together, against the LORD and against his anointed, saying,

³"Let us burst their bonds apart and cast away their cords from us."

⁴He who sits in the heavens laughs; the Lord holds them in derision.

⁵Then he will speak to them in his wrath, and terrify them in his fury, saying,

⁶"As for me, I have set my King on Zion, my holy hill."

⁷I will tell of the decree: The LORD said to me, "You are my Son; today I have begotten you.

⁸Ask of me, and I will make the nations your heritage, and the ends of the earth your possession.

⁹You shall break them with a rod of iron and dash them in pieces like a potter's vessel."

¹⁰Now therefore, O kings, be wise; be warned, O rulers of the earth.

¹¹Serve the LORD with fear, and rejoice with trembling.

¹²Kiss the Son, lest he be angry, and you perish in the way, for his wrath is quickly kindled. Blessed are all who take refuge in him.

Type of Psalm: Royal/Messianic

Structure:
1) Statement of question: Why do the nations oppose God? (v1)
2) Example of the issue (v2-3)
   Verse 1, and verses 2 and 3: synonymous parallelism
3) God's response: establishing a king/promising a victory (v8-9)
4) Instruction: repent, and serve God's son (v10-12)
   Verses 11-12: synonymous parallelism

Poetic structure:
   The Psalm begins and ends with synonymous parallelisms.
   Opening: opposition to God and its futility.
   Body: The coming triumph of Christ.
   Closing: A warning and invitation for those who are opposed to God to be reconciled with him while there is still time.

Sample sermon/lesson exegetical outline:
   Main idea: The peoples of the earth are opposed to God, but God will triumph. God's enemies can become his children if they turn unto his Son in faith.
   1) The world and nations oppose God. (Cf. Romans 1:19-31)

>   a) They want to cast off God's reign.
>   b) It is ultimately futile; they cannot prevail.
> 2) God's attitude towards the wicked.
>   a) He laughs at their folly.
>   b) He sends his Son into their midst to reign and subdue.
> 3) God's open invitation to the wicked.
>   a) Repent and believe in Christ.
>   b) The Gospel is a "limited time offer."
>   c) There will be forgiveness for the wicked who believes on the Son.
>   d) Yet, when the day of salvation ends, the son himself will judge.

Truly, the psalms are poems lovelier than trees, and far more precious than human poetry. We ought to sing them, pray them, memorize them and preach them. The hard work it takes to understand them will be richly rewarded with a depth and breadth of faith in the God who authored them. God has written songs about himself for us to sing. Let us do so.

The Song of Songs. The other major poetic book of the Bible is the Song of Solomon. It is often neglected because of what some regard as its racy content. The Reformers, too, did not know what to do with the Song of Solomon, interpreting it as an allegory of the relationship between Christ and his church. Yet, if we own the precious principles of the grammatical/historical method of interpreting the Scriptures, the door of allegory is closed to us. God speaks in plain language. And, plainly, the Song of Solomon is a song about the divine gift of marital love. It celebrates the garden of delights that is given to men and women by God in the context of the Christian marriage.

Some have argued that the Song of Songs is properly classified as wisdom literature, while noting that its structure is poetic. Thus, we have chosen to include it in the poetry section. The same rules given above for interpreting the Psalms can be brought to bear on the Song of Solomon. The Song is rich in poetic, even lurid and suggestive imagery. This has long made Christians uncomfortable. But, it ought not, because it is a celebration of the fullness of erotic love within its proper boundaries. The NIV Study Bible makes the point that the central idea of the Song of Solomon is expressed in 8:6-7:

> Set me as a seal upon your heart, as a seal upon your arm, for love is strong as death, jealousy is fierce as the grave. Its flashes are flashes of fire, the very flame of the LORD. Many waters cannot quench love, neither can floods drown it. If a man offered for love all the wealth of his house, he would be utterly despised.

Here we see that marital love is exclusive, protective, as strong as death, properly jealous for the sole affections of the other, occasionally intense and utterly invincible.

The Song of Solomon is one long love poem. It is spoken or sung by several different characters: the Lover (male), the Beloved (female), and a chorus of friends. They call to one another in turn. The story begins with an initial expression of love, the joy of their meeting, and the development of their relationship. Then, in chapter 3, a separation is introduced, and the ensuing longing and desperate search, which is quickly resolved when the woman seeks out and finds her lover. They celebrate their love for each other, and the delight they take in one another. Throughout the Song, there are nuggets of godly wise advice, such as not awakening love till its time (2:7; 3:5; 8:4), and guarding the virginal purity of young women (8:8-9).

The message of the Song of Solomon is much needed in our day, in a culture in which casual "love" surrounds us, and human sexuality knows no boundaries. It puts forward a beautiful, robust biblical vision for the beauty of human sexuality in its proper expression. God created romantic and sexual love, and did so for the bonding of man and wife in the bounds of marriage. It is a beautiful, God-given gift. Often, the church has taught about sexuality exclusively in the negative—its prohibition. But, the Song sings the delights of exclusive, reserved love as a great benefit and blessing. Therefore, we ought to teach and preach the Song and thus impress on Christians that God has attached a wonderful beauty to human sexual expression, and that is to strengthen and enliven the romantic love to be had in the bonds of godly marriage.

Chapter Six
For Crying Out Loud: Wisdom in the Bible

Wisdom cries aloud in the street, in the markets she raises her voice; at the head of the noisy streets she cries out; at the entrance of the city gates she speaks. *Proverbs 1:20-21*

Benjamin Franklin was the first media celebrity. He carefully cultivated his public image, writing "Picture me very plainly dressed, wearing my thin gray straight hair that peeps out under my only coiffure, a fine fur cap, which comes down to my forehead almost to my spectacles. Think how this must appear among the powdered heads of Paris!" Though Franklin lived his whole life in cities, Parisians swooned over the "noble frontier philosopher and simple backwoods sage."

Franklin is remembered for many things, his key role in the founding of the American republic, his scientific advances and useful inventions. Schoolchildren may still memorize proverbs from his *Poor Richard's Almanac* even today, "Early to bed, early to rise, makes a man healthy, wealthy and wise." Yet, though his Puritan upbringing haunted him throughout his life and he was a fast friend of Cotton Mather (the last living Puritan) and the fiery Calvinistic evangelist George Whitefield,

Franklin relished the role of infidel and lived a profligate life. Ben Franklin was smart, but was he wise?

Perhaps it is good to step back and ask the fundamental question: what is wisdom? Is it knowledge, or something more? Certainly, wisdom must be more than knowledge. Many brilliant people have made a shipwreck of their lives through foolish choices. Wisdom is more than simple knowledge. The Scriptures give us the definition of wisdom. First, wisdom begins with fear of the Lord: "The fear of the LORD is the beginning of wisdom; all those who practice it have a good understanding." (Psalm 111:10) Wisdom means living an obedient life in relationship with the Lord. In Proverbs 1:2-4, Solomon adds that wisdom is the ability "to understand words of insight, to receive instruction in wise dealing, in righteousness, justice, and equity; to give prudence to the simple, knowledge and discretion to the youth". In short, wisdom is simply truth put into practice, and skill at knowing how to apply true principles to the multiform situations one faces in everyday life.

Throughout the Scriptures, wisdom is contrasted with foolishness. "The fool says in his heart, 'There is no God.'" (Psalm 14:1 and 53:1) In other words, the foolish person lives a life as a practical atheist, without reference to God, as if everything that mattered existed "under the sun." And yet, if such a man looked closely enough, he would see that all he gains by his toil under the sun is utterly meaningless, because it all ends in the grave. Wisdom calls us away from foolishness to the things that really matter, the things of enduring value, and the only things that can give real meaning and purpose to life: "The end of the matter; all has been heard. Fear God and keep his commandments, for this is the whole duty of man. For God will bring every deed into judgment, with every secret thing, whether good or evil." (Ecclesiastes 12:13-14)

Thus, we must say that the Wisdom literature of the Bible (Job, Proverbs and Ecclesiastes) is some of the most practical in the Scriptures. But, because of cultural distance, many Christians balk at attempting to understand and apply the content of these books to their lives. If we would invest the effort, however, how many would be saved from the ravages of simplistic theology, foolish decisions and chasing after the wind?

Because these four books are so diverse in style, despite their similarity in content, it is necessary to take them up one at a time, and bring out some unique features and considerations of each.

Just because you're righteous doesn't mean he isn't out to get you—Job. As has often been said, Job is a theodicy—a justification of God in the face of human suffering. The question is one of timeless relevance, "If God is good, why does he allow (or ordain) bad things to happen to his people?" Or, to paraphrase C. S. Lewis, "If God sees suffering, and will not stop it, he is not good; if God sees suffering, and cannot stop it, he is not God." The book of Job answers that problem, even if, to the minds of many people, the answer is a very unsettling one.

The story line is simple. Job is a prosperous and devout servant of the Lord. The Lord mentions Job to Satan, and then allows Satan to take away everything Job has. In Job's distress, four "comforters," three of who are anything but comforting, visit him. The basic contention of at least three of them is that suffering is the inevitable indication of divine displeasure, "Job, you must have sinned or God wouldn't be doing this to you!" Job knows this cannot be true, and yet, in his own responses, shows some immaturity and misunderstanding of God. It is important to remember, in the speeches of the book of Job, that the speakers know some true things about God, many times just enough to be dangerous. Partial truths about God can be more destructive than no truths at all.

Because the speeches of Job's comforters are longer than most monologues in the Scriptures, an immature reader may be tempted to extract part of the speech as if what the speaker was saying were true. But, one must be careful especially with the speeches of Eliphaz, Bildad and Zophar (Elihu will be considered separately). *What they say in any given paragraph* may *be true about God, but is most likely distorted by the falsehood of the overall point of their monologue.* So, it is crucial here to read in context.

Truth can be morphed into falsehood if the overall point being made is false. For instance, in Job 20, Zophar makes the wicked statement that their joy is brief, but horrible judgment will come upon them. This is partially true. Yet, by reading Job's response, we can see that Zophar is mistaken: sometimes the rich continue to prosper and be blessed throughout this life. Moreover, the implication of Zophar's speech is that Job *must* be wicked, because otherwise these calamities would not have befallen him. In Zophar's eyes, earthly calamity equals divine displeasure and judgment. We must read the comforter's speeches in light of their overall point, and the response that Job makes to them.

Yet, one must also be careful with the speeches of Job. Though Job knows God more fully than most of his companions, this does not exempt him from making misstatements about God's character or doings. One can see this most clearly in the final dialogue between God and Job. Twice, early on in the book, we are told that what Job said in the preceding section was not sinful, and that he did not charge God with wrongdoing. That changes as the book progresses. Much of what Job says is true, and yet his speeches become increasingly bitter, as he pleads his righteousness before God. Job 31:35: "Oh, that I had one to hear me! (Here is my signature! Let the Almighty answer me!)"

How do we distinguish when Job was justified in what he said, and when he was impertinent, when he was right about God, and when he was mistaken? First, arguably, we ought to look at the counsel of Elihu. Many assume that Elihu's speeches are no different in character from the other three comforters. Yet, some have disputed that, and rightly so. The text gives us cues as to why.

The author of Job makes an editorial comment about Elihu in 32:2, "Then Elihu the son of Barachel the Buzite, of the family of Ram, burned with anger. He burned with anger at Job *because he justified himself rather than God.*" [Emphasis added.] There is a great difference between Elihu's speeches and those of the other comforters and Job himself. In the speeches of the first three comforters, and of Job, we find a preoccupation with the actions of man: whether he is righteous or wicked, and God is relegated to the role of a reflex actor—he is constrained to despoil evildoers, and bless the righteous. But Elihu's concern is not man-centered, but God-centered! Look at some of his exclamations about God: God is greater than man (32:12); God does not have to answer to man (32:13); God is both just and merciful (34:12ff). What is most staggering is Elihu's claim that God will redeem and justify his people by way of a Mediator (33:23-28)! One can thus see the footprints of the Suffering Servant walking through the pages of Job.

This all might remain unconvincing until one reads the Lord's verdict on the three comforters in 42:7-9. God declares that he is angry with Eliphaz, Bildad and Zophar, and that they must sacrifice to him. Who is missing from that list? Elihu—the one who points us to Christ, and God's good purposes demonstrated towards us in him.

All of this serves simply to show us the importance of reading carefully. We can pass a positive verdict on Elihu's speeches because:

1) The author of the book stresses Elihu's different and just perspective on God. (editorial comment)

2) What Elihu tells us about God comports well with what God tells us about himself in the subsequent chapters. (immediate context)

3) Elihu's doctrine of God squares with what we know about God from the rest of Scripture (overall context).

Then, and ultimately, we must look at the response of God that dominates chapters 38-42, and Job's final response. In brief, God's answer to Job was, "I am God, and you're not!" Or, as Nebuchadnezzar rightly said (Daniel 4:34b-35), "I blessed the Most High, and praised and honored him who lives forever, for his dominion is an everlasting dominion, and his kingdom endures from generation to generation; all the inhabitants of the earth are accounted as nothing, and he does according to his will among the host of heaven and among the inhabitants of the earth; and none can stay his hand or say to him, 'What have you done?'"

Job's final response in 42:5-6 gives us the conclusion and point of the book, "I had heard of you by the hearing of the ear, but now my eye sees you; therefore I despise myself, and repent in dust and ashes." Though God is God, and we're not him, and he can do with us as he pleases, yet he would have us to know him, and turn to him. The whole book of Job can be read profitably, if one reads the end of the story first!

A thoroughly depressing sermon?—Ecclesiastes. The ancient church father Tertullian quipped, "What has Athens to do with Jerusalem? Nothing!" He was speaking of the relationship of divine revelation to human philosophy. When the Gospel came to the Roman Empire, it confronted the philosophies of its day, and, in many cases, fell prey to their language and influence. Mention philosophy, and most people's eyes glaze over with bad memories of a college 101 course; philosophy is dogged by the eternal question of its relevance. It is true, much of philosophy is disconnected from everyday life; and yet, at its root, philosophy is the question of the meaning of life.

As the Monty Python comedy troupe put it, "Why are we here? What is life all about? Is God really real, or is there some doubt... Is life just a game where we make up the rules, while we're searching for something to say, or are we just simply spiraling coils of self-replicating DNA?"

Throughout the twentieth century, two equally bleak schools of thought have dominated philosophy: the nihilists and the existentialists. Nihilist philosophy could be summed up in the refrain of the song by the group Queen, "Bohemian

Rhapsody." "Nothing really matters. Nothing really matters. Nothing really matters to me." Nothing is real; nothing counts for anything; there is no significance to life whatsoever.

Existentialism is somewhat different, but not unrelated. Existentialists argue that the past is a closed book, over and done with, the future is a non-entity, and that all one has is this moment. "Seize the day!" is the cry of the existentialist. If there is any meaning to life at all, it can only be found by what one experiences in the moment, and so one ought to quest after experience. There are no consequences, and no real cause and effect relationship between events.

Nihilists and existentialist philosophers have asked the question, "Is there a purpose to all this?" and concluded, "No." No wonder so many philosophers commit suicide!

As Solomon tells us, there is truly nothing new under the sun. The same questions, and in some cases, answers or lack thereof, of the nihilists and existentialists are found in the ancient book of Ecclesiastes. Three refrains repeat themselves again and again throughout Ecclesiastes. The first is *vanity* ("meaningless!"). Solomon proceeds through every human endeavor and discovers that there is no real meaning to work, pleasure, wealth, or learning, at least not *under the sun*. Every human endeavor is *a chasing after the wind*. These three phrases are the interpretive keys to Ecclesiastes. As a general rule of biblical interpretation, it is very important to note repeated words or refrains—biblical authors use these to emphasize key points.

Ecclesiastes is an inside view into the mind of the skeptic, the one without hope and without God in the world. His life is lived "under the sun," that is, without any thought of, or reference to, a personal and loving Creator. What such a person finds is that, though there are diversions with which can occupy one's self throughout life—sex, money, career, and the like—there is no lasting happiness to be had in such things. Why? Because the grave looms large above them all.

It is important to note these three key phrases because they help the interpreter to discover the point of each narrative in Ecclesiastes. Whatever people think gives meaning to life, apart from God, is really vanity—fooling one's self. Why? Because it is chasing the elusive thing—the wind, that no one can ever catch. This is the sad life of billions who live, seek out pleasure and avoid pain, and die, be they king or pauper.

If this all seems pretty depressing, it is! The purpose is not to leave us in despair, but rather to encourage us to forsake empty things, and quest after that which gives life real significance. It is important, should one undertake to preach or teach on Ecclesiastes that the purpose of it is to critique, and not commend, the bleak worldview it sets forth in such passages. Moreover, it provides us with the alternative to such a worldview, namely a life that is lived unto God.

Thus, Ecclesiastes should be taught as posing the question of purpose, not as teaching that there indeed is no purpose. Throughout the book, rays of this purpose pierce through the gloom of human misery, but in the last chapter, life's purpose shines through in its brilliance and scatters the darkness once and for all. Though everything under the sun, considered in and of itself is meaningless, if we are connected to that which is beyond the sun, life here is filled with purpose! Ecclesiastes 12:1, 13-14, "Remember also your Creator in the days of your youth, before the evil days come and the years draw near of which you will say, 'I have no pleasure in them'...The end of the matter; all has been heard. Fear God and keep his commandments, for this is the whole duty of man. For God will bring every deed into judgment, with every secret thing, whether good or evil." The whole of the book must be preached and taught in light of its conclusion.

And, here too, we see a powerful example of why all the Scripture must be taught with reference to Christ. The worldview of Ecclesiastes is "meaningless," but Jesus came that we might have life—and have it more abundantly! It is only with reference to him that all of life becomes suffused with purpose, and we realize our chief end, namely "to glorify God, and enjoy him forever." The cure for the bleak worldview of Ecclesiastes is that the purpose of life is to glorify God, and the reward for that is not a striving after the wind, but the eternal enjoyment of God.

Rich Solomon's almanac—Proverbs. All cultures of the world have proverbs—pithy sayings meant to impart wisdom in a memorable way. Sayings like "he who lies down with dogs shall rise up with fleas" need no explanation. That is true of much of the biblical book of Proverbs—simple sayings that give wisdom.

Yet, there is a marked difference between the worldly aphorisms of various cultures and the proverbs of the Scripture. While most worldly wisdom is simply concerned with coping in the world, Biblical wisdom is concerned, first of all, with a life lived in the presence of God. At the very outset of Proverbs, we are told Proverbs 1:7, "The fear of the Lord is the beginning of knowledge; fools despise wisdom and instruction."

There are two principles necessary to interpreting Proverbs. The first is to understand wisdom and folly. Wisdom and folly are the two poles of Proverbs. They are not identical to righteousness and wickedness, but neither are they unrelated. Often, foolishness leads one down the path towards wickedness, but some things in life are simply unwise without being, in and of themselves, sinful. Wisdom is often defined as "knowledge (or truth) rightly applied." In short, it is knowing how to apply rightly the principles of the Scripture to the myriad of different situations one faces in life. Folly is the opposite of wisdom: it is failing to apply truth to life—fools despise wisdom and discipline. A fool may know the truth; it just doesn't do him any good. Often, he is simply too lazy to apply the truth, favoring instant gratification over the long-term benefits of moral uprightness.

The other has already been related but bears repeating: we must distinguish between proverbs, promises and precepts. In short, a proverb is not a commandment. It is rather a piece of wise advice that must be tailored to each individual situation in life. One can see this clearly contrasting Proverbs 26:4, "Answer not a fool according to his folly, lest you be like him yourself" with the immediate succeeding verse, 26:5, "Answer a fool according to his folly, lest he be wise in his own eyes." Is that a contradiction? No. Each applies in a different situation. That, in fact, is the essence of wisdom—knowing how to apply truth to life. Thus, Proverbs must be read as a whole collection, each balanced against the other, and each applied rightly in any given situation.

If proverbs are not precepts, neither are they promises. They are rather general principles: a righteous person is more likely to live a long life than a wicked one (10:27), but this does not deny that many good people meet an early death. Proverbs are, in short, sanctified common sense, and they need to be read that way, not as binding promises that, if we do "A," the result must inevitably be "B."

We must remember, too, that Proverbs are written in the cultural language of their day, and the idiom needs to be translated. For instance, Proverbs 25:24, "It is better to live in a corner of the housetop than in a house shared with a quarrelsome wife." Ancient Judean housetops had flat roofs on which the occupants slept during hot weather. We might update it by saying, "It's better to live in a shed than to share a mansion obtained by marrying a bitter woman."

In summary, Gordon D. Fee and Douglas Stewart give the following helpful principles for interpreting Proverbs:

1) Proverbs are often figurative, pointing beyond themselves.
2) Proverbs are practical, not theoretical and theological.
3) Proverbs are memorable, not precise.
4) Proverbs do not teach materialism, but spiritual reward.

5) Proverbs that use ancient idiom may need to be updated to current situations.
6) Proverbs are not promises, but guidelines for good behavior.
7) Proverbs may exaggerate or use other literary devices to make a point, and thus must not be read in a hyper-literal fashion.
8) Proverbs give good advice, but not exhaustive recommendations.
9) The right use of proverbs is to provide practical advice for wise daily living.

If one remembers these principles, he can read and teach the wise life that Proverbs commends, and that is so sorely needed in the church today.

In closing, the Godly life is to be wisely lived. God has given us the tools to live a wise, and thus productive and joyful, life by fearing him and keeping his commandments. It is utterly imperative that this be taught in the churches today, when so many people are making a shipwreck of their lives simply because nobody ever taught them how to apply biblical wisdom to the choices they face. That is the calling of the Bible teacher—he is to help his people live a life that is wholly given over to God, and thus far more productive and happy than the life that is lived for sin and self.

Chapter Seven
"Thus Says the Lord": The Prophets

Any good dictionary will tell you that a prophet is someone who foretells the future. It is just doing its job of describing what people usually mean by the term. A better dictionary will have a second meaning as well: one who speaks to men to reveal a divine message. This second definition is the biblical meaning of the word. In both the Old and New Testaments, a prophet was a person to whom God entrusted a message for his people. The word "prophet" comes from a compound Greek word meaning "speak before". Thus, in a very real sense, a prophet stood before God to deliver his message to his people. For this reason, some writers describe him as an ambassador from God, the great King, to his earthly nation Israel, or to other nations.

One thing to note quickly here, and to discuss more thoroughly below, is that the prophetic writings were addressed to particular people at particular times in particular situations. The majority of the content of the message concerned that time and that situation. Even the predictive portion consisted mostly of warnings or promises for a time that was in the near future to the hearers. One should be extremely wary of attempting to apply an Old Testament prophecy to our own time or to our own future. Such prophecies do occur, but are rare.

In the narrative portions of the Old Testament, we read much about the prophets, particularly the early ones. Most of what we read tells us what they did and what happened to them. Such passages are to be interpreted, as is any narrative material. Occasionally, a passage describes a message they delivered. When this occurs, there is seldom a problem with interpretation. Both the historical and literary contexts are plainly before us, and it is a relatively easy task to keep them in mind as we seek to understand the message. These prophecies frequently give us useful examples, but seldom does our context match theirs sufficiently to receive the message as a direct statement to ourselves.

For example, in 1 Samuel 13, the prophet Samuel rebuked King Saul for not waiting for Samuel, as he had been instructed, and offering a burnt offering on his own. This was contrary to the Mosaic law of the offerings, so Samuel told Saul that his kingdom would not be passed down to his descendents, but given to a man after God's own heart (David). Samuel's prophecy was not directed to us. Saul was a king: we are not. Saul was under the Mosaic ceremonial law: we are not. There is no way in which this prophecy could apply to us. Yet this incident does give us an example of the seriousness with which God takes his word and the foolishness of deliberately ignoring God's instructions.

On the other hand, we could look at a New Testament passage, Acts 17. The Philippian jailer was panic-stricken when an earthquake opened up the prison. He was amazed when the prisoners did not attempt to escape. He recognized that the disciples had something that he needed in his life, and asked, "Sirs, what must I do to be saved?" Paul was certainly filling the function of a prophet in declaring to him the word of God, "Believe in the Lord Jesus, and you shall be saved, you and your household."

Does that prophetic message apply to us? Look at the literary context. There is no indication there whether this statement is of specific or general application. Look at the historical context. This man was a jailer, living in first-century Philippi. We are of many professions, living in various cities in the twenty-first century. Do any of these differences prevent the message from applying to us? We all know that the answer to that question is "no." But how do we know that? Not from this passage in itself, but from the multitude of didactic, or teaching passages within the New Testament which teach us the same thing, such as Romans 3:22 or 10:11, or Galatians 3:22, or Ephesians 2:8, 9.

The previous example shows an application of the analogy of faith described in Chapter Two. In order to find the meaning of this message for us, we had to refer to other passages of Scripture, which clearly were intended to teach us the lesson that Paul spoke to the jailer. Prophecy tends to be given in figurative language, using images of unusual creatures, places or situations to describe the truth. It tends to be addressed to people who are in a very different historical context than ourselves. Because of this, the hermeneutical process of finding either the original meaning or its meaning to us often requires us to refer to other passages: narrative and, especially, didactic passages where the language may be clearer and the application more direct.

In contrast to the prophets found in the narrative books, there were sixteen prophets whose messages have been collected and compiled into books of the Old Testament. These books consist primarily of the oracles, or messages that the prophets proclaimed, while telling us little of what happened to them (except perhaps, for Daniel and Jonah). This fact adds to the necessity of referring to other Scripture to aid us in interpreting their messages in their historical context. Before beginning a study of a passage in a prophetic book, it is helpful to refer to a commentary or a Bible dictionary to learn about the circumstances under which the prophet labored and which he addressed. Although it should not replace the use of other references, The table at the end of this chapter provides a quick reference, giving for each prophet the approximate time of his labor, those to whom he prophesied, and the name(s) of the king(s) during that period.

The fact that the first four of these books are called the "major prophets" and the latter twelve are called "minor prophets" has nothing to do with their relative importance. Rather, it simply refers to the length of the books. The twelve minor prophets together form a volume about the size of any one of the four major prophets. The minor prophets are every bit as rich per page as the major prophets. Indeed, a quick look at the words of Jesus as recorded by Luke will show that He either quoted or referred to a saying of one of the minor prophets almost as often as one of the major prophets.

God sent his great prophet Moses to Israel to be the covenant mediator between Him and the nation of Israel. Moses proclaimed God's law to the people (Exodus 19:7) and he brought back their agreement to the Lord (Exodus 19:8). Throughout his life, he functioned as their leader, but always in this mediatorial capacity. In Deuteronomy 27 and 28, Moses organized an elaborate ritual to proclaim to the twelve tribes the blessings of obedience to God's law and the curses of disobedience.

Of course, even in that law proclaimed by Moses, there was provision for forgiveness. This was the model of the prophetic message throughout the Old Testament. Whether a prophet functioned during the period of the judges, the kings of the northern or southern kingdom, the exile, or even later, the burden of the message was the blessing of obedience, the curse of disobedience and the Lord's gracious provision for restoration.

Different prophets emphasized different parts of the message. The message was given in their own words, using their own illustrations (although always inspired by the Holy Spirit). But it was always from the same God to the same people to proclaim the same covenant.

The prophets were not a class of people with special ability to perceive the circumstances and predict the future accordingly. They were the first to admit this. Rather, their ability to recognize sin for what it was, and to foretell the future was entirely through the revelation God gave them. The prophets themselves ranged from educated men (Haggai) to sheepherders (Amos), but they all used similar language. Over and over they use phrases such as "Thus says the Lord of hosts", "the Lord said to me, 'Go prophesy to My people Israel'", "hear the word of the Lord". Almost every one of the sixteen prophetic books begins with a phrase explaining that this is the word of the Lord. The few that do not begin this way also say the same sort of thing within the early verses.

The fact that the prophets spoke the word of the Lord is dramatically illustrated by two incidents. In Numbers 22-24, Balaam really wanted to please one of Israel's enemies, Balak, and make a pile of money. Balak hired him to curse Israel, but twice, when he tried to do it, he blessed them instead. Balak, of course, was angry, but Balaam answered, (24:13 NAS) "Though Balak were to give me his house full of silver and gold, I could not do anything contrary to the command of the LORD…What the LORD speaks, that will I speak."

We are all familiar with Jonah, whom the Lord commanded to call Nineveh to repentance. Try as he might, he was not able to avoid going to

Nineveh and proclaiming the Lord's oracle of repentance to them. He hated to do it so much that he was angry when they did repent. Yet he was not able to speak other than the word of the Lord.

One other characteristic of the prophetic books complicates the task of interpreting them. That is, they were not spoken at one time or one place. Rather, each book is a collection of the oracles, or prophetic messages, given by that prophet, sometimes over years of service. Sometimes, this collection was written by the prophet himself, and sometimes it was written by someone else, always under the guidance of the Holy Spirit. Because of this, it can sometimes be difficult to isolate individual oracles in order to consider them separately from other messages brought by the same prophet. Yet, if we are to properly understand the message, we have to determine, as nearly as possible, where that oracle begins and ends.

Where other genres of Scripture are properly studied in terms of paragraphs, the prophetic books are most profitably studied in terms of the oracles. The use of a commentary is probably the best way to identify the individual oracles. Yet we do not have to be completely dependent on the work of others. There are clues within the text, which we can easily identify. Usually, the clue will be an introductory statement. A few of these clues are discussed below.

"Thus says the Lord..." or "The word of the Lord came unto me..." or a similar expression is a common prophetic introduction to an oracle. Although it is not an infallible indication, it is a common way for the prophet to begin a new message. Occasionally, a prophet used such an expression as a means of emphasis, but unless the following words are clearly an extension of the preceding words, it would be expected that a new oracle is being introduced. The book of Amos uses this form almost exclusively.

"Woe..." is used by Habakkuk, Micah and Zephaniah to introduce the "woe oracle", an announcement of imminent distress and doom, together with the reason for it. Although many oracles told the hearers of their sin and the punishment that would follow, the woe oracle lends urgency to the message. Joel used the word "wail" for the same purpose.

Several of the prophets present an oracle in the form of a lawsuit against God's people for their infidelity. An illustration of this is found in Micah 6. "Arise, plead your case...Listen to the indictment of the Lord...Because the Lord has a case against his people." By putting the accusation of lawlessness into the setting of a law court, the seriousness of the situation is emphasized. Israel was well aware of the fate of those who were found guilty by a court of justice.

But, the story is not complete without considering the oracles of promise. The oracles considered above had their purpose in forcing God's people to recognize their sin and to repent. By themselves they could instill a feeling of hopelessness, so here is where the oracle of promise functioned. In the midst of trouble, or even in the anticipation of it, the Lord sent his prophets with a message of hope for the future.

Micah 7 is an interesting chapter in this regard. The chapter begins with a "woe" oracle. The corruption of God's people is pictured, occasionally in courtroom language, but the woe described is more the result of living in a lawless land than of God's judgment. The woe of judgment is confined to verse 9, "I will bear the indignation of the Lord because I have sinned against Him..." It is immediately followed by "...until He pleads my case and executes justice for me." Israel's enemies will be judged and made desolate. The chapter concludes with a declaration of the love and forgiveness of the Lord. Even though they were headed for judgment, God's people were given hope.

The oracle of promise was especially characteristic of the prophets during the exile in Babylon. Just prior to the captivity, Jeremiah prophesied that the captivity would last 70 years, after which Judah would be restored (25:11, 12; 29:10). It is interesting to note that Daniel was not given this information directly by the Lord as a revelation, but learned it in his reading of Jeremiah (Dan. 9:2). Although Ezekiel begins with oracles of desolation against Judah for her wickedness, it turns to oracles against her enemies. Then, mixed with the oracles against her enemies, we find promises of restoration for God's flock.

Finally, Ezekiel, together with Jeremiah and Daniel, turns to promises of a glorious future. In accordance with these prophecies, Jerusalem was restored. The temple was rebuilt and the sacrifices reestablished. Almost all commentators see oracles in these books, which go far beyond this restoration and point toward this Messianic age or to the end times. Herein lies a problem, because the commentators do not agree on the interpretation. They range from almost skeptical unbelief to fanciful imagination. It is at this point that it becomes necessary to rely upon a trusted commentary for guidance. Even so, it is not necessary to completely give up thinking for one's self.

Some of these oracles are explained in the New Testament. For example, the New Covenant prophesied in Jeremiah 31:31-34 is plainly shown in Hebrews 8:8-12 to be that better covenant whose Mediator is Christ, our Lord. It is to be claimed as our own. The new heart promised in Ezekiel 11:19 and 36:26 is fulfilled in Romans 2:29 and 2 Corinthians 3:3. The return of Elijah promised in Malachi 4:5 is explained by our Lord in Matthew 11:14 to refer to John the Baptizer.

Some of these oracles are not explicitly interpreted in the New Testament, but from our New Testament perspective, we can see the meaning with reasonable clarity. For example, Ezekiel's prophecy of the valley of the dry bones probably gave much comfort to the Jews as a picture of having a new life in Jerusalem after the living death of exile in Babylon. But how clearly it illustrates the process of spiritual rebirth, when one dead in sin is reborn by the Spirit and given spiritual life. (Remember, the Hebrew word for spirit could also mean wind or breath.) Of course, others have associated it with the resurrection from the dead at the last day, an interpretation that also has validity.

In a similar way, the later chapters of Ezekiel describe a new temple. No temple matching this description was ever built by the repatriated Jews.

"Thus Says the Lord": The Prophets

Because of this, some commentators expect such a literal temple to be rebuilt in the last days by a reestablished Israel. However, the New Testament makes it clear that the temple, as God's dwelling place with his people now, is in their hearts, both individually (2 Corinthians 6:16) and collectively (Ephesians 2:21). Ezekiel, by God's inspiration, gave a wonderful picture of God's closeness to his people and he gave it in verbal images, which were very familiar to the Jews of that day.

The final chapters of Daniel have also been used to form elaborate programs of expected happenings in the end times. They describe wars. Jesus Himself has told us that these days will be filled with "wars and rumors of wars." (Matthew 24:6) But we are specifically told that it is useless to try to predict the details of the end times from these sayings. In 12:9 (NAS), Gabriel tells Daniel that these words of prophecy are concealed and sealed up "until the end time." The wicked will never understand them, but the righteous will recognize these things. In the meantime, we would do better concentrating on those things in God's word which we can understand now.

Do You Understand What You Are Reading?

The Prophets

Prophet	~ B.C.	People	King(s)
Isaiah	735-690	Judah	Uzziah, Jotham, Ahaz, Hezekiah
Jeremiah	627-585	Judah	Josiah thru Zedekiah
Ezekiel	593-573	Exiles	
Daniel	605-536	Exiles	
Hosea	760-725	Israel	Jeroboam II thru Hoshea
Joel	800?	Judah	Joash?
Amos	760	Various	Jeroboam II, Uzziah
Obadiah	520?	Edom	Post-Exile?
Jonah	750	Ninevah	
Micah	740-735	Both	Jotham, Ahaz, Pekah
Nahum	720	Ninevah	
Habakkuk	600?	Babylon	
Zephaniah	630	Judah	Josiah
Haggai	520	Post-Exile	
Zechariah	520-490	Post-Exile	
Malachi	440	Post-Exile	

Chapter Eight
God Became Man: The Gospels

At first glance, it might seem that the Gospels are simply narrative material, with teaching passages included. Therefore, we should only have to add some principles of the study of Jesus' teaching to the principles we have already seen for narrative passages. But that is quite an oversimplification. In the first place, there are four Gospels, with many similarities and also with differences. Why? The answer to that question will have an important effect on our understanding of them.

In the second place, the Gospels contain a lot of teaching material. These teachings were given in a different way and for a different purpose than were the Epistles, for example. This must be taken into account in our study of them. Thirdly, in the "upper level" story (discussed in Chapter Three), the Gospels present the climax of God's redemptive work. They take us from the promise of redemption to its accomplishment. Finally, we have to account for the difference in emphasis between the "synoptic" Gospels (Matthew, Mark and Luke) and the Gospel of John.

It must be recognized at the outset that the Gospels are not biographies of our Lord Jesus. They make no attempt to be a comprehensive, sequential account of his life. Rather, each of the Gospel writers has selected and organized his material in order to emphasize a particular point of view; all, of course, under the guidance of the Holy Spirit. It is probably better not to try to find an exact timeline of the incidents described in the Gospels. If it were of great importance, the Gospels would have been written that way. Of more importance is the emphasis of each of the Gospel writers. A good study Bible will have an introduction to each of the Gospels, which will probably give an insight into this.

It is generally agreed that Mark was the first of the Gospels to be written. This is the nearest to a true biography. It is an action Gospel, using the word "immediately" repeatedly. It seems to have been written simply to present the facts about the ministry and teaching of Jesus. Except for his quotation from Malachi in his description of John the Baptist, Mark never explains why something occurs unless Jesus explains it in one of his teachings. Yet his vivid descriptions of Jesus' miracles and his selection of the sayings of Jesus leave no doubt as to the power of Jesus, the Son of God.

Luke, the Gentile Physician, tells us that his purpose in writing his Gospel was to enable his friend, Theophilus, (and presumably others) to have good knowledge of his faith. This Gospel complements Acts as a two-volume account of the

Savior of Jew and Gentile. He shows Jesus' tender regard for the Samaritans (10:33 and 17:13). His medical orientation shows in his accounts of the healing miracles of Jesus. He is careful to show Jesus' concern for the poor, the sick, the powerless, in both his teaching and his miracles.

Matthew's Gospel is largely organized and written to show Jesus as the fulfillment of the prophecies of the Redeemer-King, given to Israel. Repeatedly, we find the words, "…that it might be fulfilled which was spoken of by the prophet." Even in his accounts of the teachings of Jesus, he repeatedly quotes Him as telling how He fulfills prophecy.

Two themes predominate in John's Gospel. One is the presentation of Jesus as God the Son. Right in the first chapter, he presents Jesus as the Word, which was with God and was God. At the end of chapter 20, he says that this Gospel was written that we might believe the Jesus is the Christ, the Son of God. Over and over, John shows that Jesus and his Father are one. John also gives us an insight into Jesus' heart of love in an intensely personal way that none of the other Gospels attempts.

Although recognition of the several emphases of the four Evangelists can help us to understand the differences in their descriptions of the same event or discourse, we must remember that they are all telling about the same Jesus, his actions and his teachings.

Do You Understand What You Are Reading?

Whenever we set out to study a passage in one of the Gospels, it is always good to compare it with the corresponding passages in the other Gospels, when they exist. In this way, even the differences in the descriptions can help us to understand what the meaning of the passage is, within the context of the Gospel we are studying.

For example, all four Gospels relate the feeding of the five thousand. (Matt. 14:13ff; Mark 6:30ff; Luke 9:10ff; John 6:1ff.) Matthew tells us that, upon hearing of the death of John the Baptist, Jesus departed to a lonely place. Mark and Luke tell us that, upon the return of the Apostles from their missionary journey, Jesus told them to come apart for rest. From the comparison of these different accounts, we see that, even in the grief of losing his cousin, friend and herald, Jesus was concerned for the well-being of his disciples in their fatigue. Only in John do we find that Jesus used the provisions brought by a young boy to accomplish his miracle, or that it was Andrew who brought the boy to Jesus, or that Jesus was concerned not to lose a scrap of the food which his miracle had provided.

As in all biblical narrative, the fact that a certain action is described does not make it right or wrong, unless the description is accompanied by a teaching (which is often the case in the Gospels). Even if the propriety or impropriety is plain in the account, we must recognize that it occurred within a specific context, and we must be very careful in trying to apply such an example in any other context. Of course, we can be sure that any action of Jesus was right. But even then, we must consider context.

There is a movement which, to determine what should be our own response to a situation, concentrates on the question, "What would Jesus do?" A better question might be, "What would Jesus have me do?" The reason for this is simple: He was both God and man; we are mere men. He was King; we are his people. His mission on earth was to redeem his people; our mission is to serve and glorify Him. Nevertheless, both questions usually have the same answer. After all, we are being conformed to his image. Yet we cannot assume that the answers are the same in any particular instance.

For example, all four Gospels relate the cleansing of the temple by Jesus. (Matt. 21:12; Mark 11:15; Luke 19:45; John 2:13.) From Jesus' condemnation of the merchants and moneychangers for changing the temple from a "house of prayer" to a "house of merchandise" or a "den of thieves", most interpreters infer that the church should not carry on commercial activities. Of course, one can differentiate between the temple and the church, but he cannot deny that the church is a "house of prayer". How this applies to the church today is interpreted in various ways. Is it proper to charge for the cost of a congregational meal? Or for Sunday School or Bible study materials? What if such payment is voluntary? May a church youth group hold a Saturday afternoon car wash to earn money for a mission project?

This example illustrates two things. First, the context is important. Trying to apply this clear example of Jesus' actions in the temple to the context of the modern-day church can be very difficult, and we are going to have to have patience with those whose interpretation differs from our own. Second, it is evident that, when faced with some questionable situation of this type, we are not to follow Jesus' example, overturning the collection plate, making a whip of cords, and driving out the deacons. We are not infallible, sinless kings.

When we turn to the study of Jesus' teachings, as described to us in the Gospels, we face additional problems. It is just as important to consider the context of his teachings as that of his actions. But in addition, we must consider the style of his teaching, particularly his use of figures of speech. A good teacher will do much more than simply state facts—that is an effective way to put his hearers to sleep. He will also relate those facts to his hearers' experience and affections. In modern times, this is often done with illustrations on an overhead projector or computer monitor. Of course, these teaching aids were not available in Jesus' time. So Jesus, the master teacher, used language, including figures of speech, to plant visual illustrations in the minds of his hearers. These verbal devices included metaphor, simile, hyperbole and parables. We must be careful not to allow our conviction of verbal plenary inspiration to blind us to such teaching methods.

A metaphor is a form of comparison in which the illustration is presented in place of its object. For example, in Luke 13:32, when some Pharisees warned Jesus that Herod wanted to kill Him, Jesus replied, "Go and tell that fox, 'Behold, I cast out demons...'" Of course, Jesus was not saying that Herod was a four-footed beast instead of a man. He was simply painting a one-word picture of Herod as a sly, predatory, destructive person. All of that in a one-word image that his hearers could not have missed. Another example would be found in John 10:27, where Jesus said, "My sheep hear my voice..." Jesus was not speaking of wooly, four-legged creatures. Not long before this statement, Jesus had told a parable comparing Himself to a shepherd and his people to his sheep. By this metaphor, Jesus, with just one word, recalled all of the teaching of that parable. Does such a use of metaphor detract from the inerrancy of Scripture? Of course not! Rather, it increases the effectiveness of its teaching.

A simile also compares one object with another, but it does so by explicitly saying that the object is like its illustration. For example, in Matt. 17:20, Jesus speaks of having faith as a grain of mustard seed.

He could have simply called it a very small faith, but, by comparing it to the tiny seed of the mustard plant, He gave a vivid illustration of the effectiveness of even very small but true faith. Being more explicit in its comparison, the simile is less likely than the metaphor to cause confusion in the mind of the hearer who is not prepared for such a figure of speech, but also it lacks the shock value of the vivid comparison by substitution.

Hyperbole may be the most difficult of these figures of speech to place in its proper literary context. In our own time, exaggeration is so often used with at least some intent to deceive (for example in advertising) that it has taken on a somewhat suspicious connotation. It has even received the nickname "hype", as building up the qualities of a product far beyond their actual value. This is not the traditional use of the word. One dictionary defines the word as "exaggeration for effect, not meant to be taken literally." This is the traditional sense of the word, and it is the sense in which Jesus used this figure of speech. It can be a powerful teaching tool.

One example of hyperbole in Jesus' teaching, often chosen as an example, is found in Matt. 5:29-30, where Jesus says to tear out an eye or cut off a hand that causes one to sin. It is an extremely effective way of teaching that we should be willing to give up anything, any relationship, any habit that leads us into sin. Living a life that is pleasing to God is worth any sacrifice.

Another example of Jesus' use of hyperbole, perhaps even clearer than the previous one, is found in Luke 14:26, "If anyone comes to me and does not hate his own father and mother and wife and children and brothers and sisters, yes, and even his own life, he cannot be my disciple." Could Jesus really have meant that we should hate all these people? Impossible! In the first place, that would violate the Fifth Commandment, "Honor thy father and thy mother." In the second place, it would violate his own teaching elsewhere, as in his new commandment "that you love one another, even as I have loved you." Rather, his use of the word "hate" is an hyperbolic expression indicating emphatically that our love for anyone or anything should never interfere with our love for Him.

The final figure of speech, or teaching device, that Jesus commonly used is the parable. A parable is a short, fictional story, the purpose of which is to teach a lesson. Jesus used parables so often and in so many ways that we could easily devote a whole chapter to this subject. Here we will consider just a few, of the scores of parables Jesus used, in an effort to develop some principles for the study of them. Particularly, we will select several to illustrate aspects of the definition given above.

Some of Jesus' parables are so short as to be almost similes. One such is found in Matt. 13:33 (NAS), the parable of the leaven, which consists of one sentence: "The kingdom of heaven is like leaven, which a woman took, and hid in three pecks of meal, until it was all leavened." This is certainly short. It is fictional in the sense that, although it had occurred many times, Jesus was not speaking of any one particular incident. It teaches a lesson, and the lesson is the whole purpose of the telling. Therefore, our primary concern in the interpretation of a parable must be the comprehension of that lesson. In this case, a comparison with Luke 13:20 (cited in marginal notes of a good study Bible) is helpful in showing us that the "kingdom of heaven" and the "kingdom of God" are equivalent. The lesson is clear: God's sovereign rule over the affairs of this world is not something that can be seen as it happens. But we can be sure his purpose will be accomplished.

Another, longer kingdom parable is found across the page at Matt. 13:24. Here we find the parable of the wheat and the tares. Being a kingdom parable, we know that it deals with God's sovereign rule. But, being considerably longer, this parable contains many more concepts. It deals with a farmer, good seed, bad seed, a field, an enemy, germination, servants and a harvest. Each of these elements adds to the drama of the story and makes the lesson more forceful. Nevertheless, in our task of interpreting the parable, we must resist the temptation to concentrate on the details and keep our attention on the intended lesson. Obviously, the good seed and the bad seed are the children of God and the children of the devil. They grow up together and the servants (church leaders? individuals? Don't press the details: if the shoe fits, wear it.) are told not to try to root out the weeds for the danger of harming the wheat. After the harvest, they will be separated. Here we find the lesson expressed. It may look like evil prospers more than the good. (Aren't the weeds always bigger than the grass? But don't press the details.) But God's righteous judgment will be made clear at his own time.

Notice that an excessive attention to the details in themselves, rather than in their contribution to the lesson, can easily lead us into error. In this parable, one could notice that the enemy sowed the bad seed while the farmer slept. Pressing this detail beyond its intended purpose could lead us into concluding that the Devil took God by surprise when he introduced sin into the world. That, of course, would be a gross misinterpretation. By placing too much emphasis on the account of the harvest, one might conclude that, at the end time, the wicked will be gathered before the righteous. Again, that would be reading into the parable something that was never intended. After all, since the time of Christ until the end of the age, most of us will be "harvested" long before that last day.

Perhaps one exception to the definition of a parable given above might be noted in the parable of the prodigal son in Luke 15:11-32. Whereas all of the other parables teach one lesson upon which we should concentrate our attention, this parable teaches two lessons. After Jesus had so dramatically illustrated God's attitude toward the repentant sinner by the loving reception the father gave to the son who had mistreated him so badly, He continued with a second lesson. He told of the unloving heart of the older brother as an illustration of that self-satisfied attitude, which we should be careful to avoid having toward the repentant sinner. But then, perhaps we should not be too surprised at finding an exception to a man-made definition or rule. As a practical observation, it might be noted that careful attention to the lesson of the parable is the way in which this double lesson is most surely noticed.

In spite of the exception noted above (and possibly others), you can be sure that paying careful attention to the principles given in this chapter will greatly increase your understanding of both the actions and teachings of our Lord Jesus, while serving to prevent you from arriving at erroneous conclusions. Through such study, you will certainly increase both in your personal spiritual growth and in your service to your Lord.

Chapter Nine
"Dear Christian": The Epistles

> On a day like today [w]e passed the time away [w]riting love letters in the sand...
> *Words by Nick and Charles Kenny;*
> *Music by J. Fred Coots*

Each of the Epistles was written from a heart of Christian love for the reader, so in that sense, they could be called love letters, but (unlike the popular Pat Boone song) they were certainly not written in the sand for the next tide to erase. They have endured even to our own day as a part of Scripture, which we can study to our everlasting benefit. The Epistles belong to that Scriptural genre which is most specifically devoted to teaching and exhortation: the didactic passages. For this reason, they are particularly useful in our study of doctrine (teaching), behavior and church government. Of course, we can learn much about these things from other passages of the Bible, and those sources must not be neglected, but nowhere else do we find such a concentration of detailed teaching and exhortation.

There is great variety in the Epistles or letters of the New Testament. Some are addressed to an individual, others to a particular church, still others to the church as a whole or to a large portion of it.

Some are highly formal and organized, such as Hebrews and some of the Pauline Epistles, while others are very informal and abbreviated. However, they all have this in common: they were written to correct either a theological problem or to exhort the recipient to a pattern of behavior which would be pleasing to the Lord. In the latter case, it might be to correct faulty, even scandalous behavior as in the letters to the Corinthians, or to encourage the recipient to grow even stronger in his service to the Lord as in the letters to Timothy and Titus. Thus, by their very nature, they are occasional documents. That is, each one was written to address a specific situation.

The very richness of the teaching found in these letters makes it all the more necessary to study them carefully, paying particular attention to the principles which were set forth in the introductory chapters of this book. Remember: it is our aim, in studying these letters, to find out what God has said through these writers, what these words meant to the recipients and, only finally, how this meaning affects us in our own cultural context.

Let us assume, for example, that we wish to study a particular passage in order to prepare a lesson or a sermon. This passage might be a sentence of a few verses or an entire paragraph. Although the first step of the detailed study is exegesis, or determining what the passage actually says, it might be helpful to begin with the context. Read the entire letter at one time in each of at least two translations. After all, each letter was intended to be read through as a unit. In a good study Bible or commentary, find out as much as possible about the people and situation to which the letter was addressed. Outline the letter (your study Bible may already do this for you). Try to analyze each argument given in order to understand the writer's reasoning.

This preliminary process can profitably be done in the following way (although you may find another procedure helpful). First, pray for the guidance of the Holy Spirit in your study. Next, learn about the recipients and the situation that is addressed to establish the historical context. Of course, some of this will become obvious in your reading of the letter. But knowing about the people and their particular need beforehand will help you put yourself in their place and, as you read, to understand how the letter speaks to that need in that historical context. Then read the letter.

Next, read it again in another translation, this time taking notes to outline it. It is to be hoped that your study Bible or your commentary will have an outline. If so, check it. It may or may not agree with yours, but that is not important. The main thing is that you will have gotten a clear understanding of the purpose and organization of the letter, and thus you have begun to establish the literary context of the passage.

As important as the historical context is to our interpretation of a letter, the literary context is of far greater importance. For this reason, it is necessary to study paragraphs, rather than verses. But first, it is advisable to put the paragraph of concern in its proper context by studying carefully, not only the paragraph under analysis, but also the preceding and succeeding paragraphs, looking carefully for connections between the thoughts of each. It is advisable to continue to keep notes during this detailed study. They may be useful in remembering this context during the process of interpreting the key paragraph.

The first step in the actual interpretation is to determine, as exactly as possible, what the passage really says (exegesis). Here, we have to rely on the translators. Read the passage in several translations. (If the translations disagree on a word, consult an interlinear Greek New Testament and a Greek-English lexicon to gain a better insight into the sentence than if the disagreement had not occurred. Or, we can consult a trusted commentary.)

Analyze each sentence grammatically. Try to determine the subject of each clause, the antecedent of each pronoun (to whom is the word "he" referring?), the tense of each verb (The New American Standard Bible is particularly careful in this regard.), paying close attention to the prepositions used (to, by, through, in, etc.). If there is the slightest doubt as to the meaning of a word, look it up in a good dictionary. In other words, take the time to be sure you are seeing, as accurately as possible, the thoughts contained in the words on the page. In this step, there are two occasions to use a good commentary: (1) when you are really stuck, after plenty of effort, and (2) when you have finished and want to check your work. If the commentary disagrees with your exegesis, reconsider your work, but don't just assume that the commentary must be right. Even the best commentaries have questionable points. Check another one, if it is available. Ask a trusted advisor. Just be sure the matter is resolved in your mind, even if you do eventually accept the commentary's position.

The next step is interpretation proper. The question to be answered is, "What does this passage mean?" We want to determine the thoughts, the teachings, the exhortations, which the writer was expressing through the words. Of course, this begins with the results of the first step: the meaning of the words used and their grammatical interrelations. In the great majority of cases, that literal, lexical, grammatical process results in the correct understanding of the passage.

The first principle to be observed is the analogy of faith. Scripture will not contradict itself. What it states to be true in one context will always be true in another context. If it seems to be otherwise, we must be interpreting something wrongly. Of course, to catch such a problem can require a good acquaintance with Scripture, in order to make the necessary comparison. Let us consider a compact example where, within a few verses, a seeming conflict can arise. This would be found in the opening verses of Galatians 6, where verse 2 tells us to "bear one another's burdens," and verse 5 says, "For each one shall bear his own burden." The same situation is found in different translations. The NIV, very properly, uses the word "burden" in verse 2 and "load" in verse 5, but the meaning of these words is still close enough to present a problem.

The answer to the dilemma can be found in the context of the two verses. In the first case, Paul had been instructing those Galatians who were mature in the faith to help a fellow believer who was struggling with some sin in his life. By gentle rebuke, advice, correction and helpfulness they would be helping him to bear the burden of overcoming that sin. In that sense, they would be "bearing his burden."

In verses 3 and 4, Paul turns specifically to the sin of pride. How easy it is to deceive ourselves into thinking of ourselves too highly! It is easy to think that the wonderful things that have happened to us have come about because of our own wisdom or strength or faithfulness. So, in verse 5, Paul says that the burden of proof is on ourselves to prove the ground of our boasting. We find, then, that the conviction of the consistency of Scripture forced upon our attention a contextual problem, which might have been missed otherwise.

But even here, this may not be finding the full expression of Paul's lesson. Remember that we spoke of attention to the larger context. Particularly, we have recommended attention to the preceding and following paragraphs. If we follow that procedure here, our attention is drawn to the last verse of the previous chapter (Gal. 5:26 NAS), where Paul says, "Let us not become boastful, challenging one another, envying one another." It is hard to imagine Paul reproving boastfulness and yet allowing it within the same extended context, as long as the boaster makes sure he really has something to boast about. It makes more sense to understand Paul to be speaking ironically in verse 5, knowing that an honest self-examination would convince any believer that it is only by the power of the Holy Spirit that any of us can accomplish any good thing. "Sola Deo gloria!" To God alone be the glory!

The previous example has dealt with attention both to the analogy of faith and to the literary context of a passage or even of a word. Yet, even though it is secondary to these considerations, we must also pay attention to the cultural or historical context of the letter. An interesting example of the interplay of these considerations can be found in 1 Corinthians 11:1-16. In this passage, Paul bases his instructions at one point on the creation order and, at another point, on local custom. Without going into a detailed analysis of the passage, it would be well to consider one teaching from the passage, which has caused much disagreement in the church over the years. This teaching deals with the propriety of a woman wearing a head covering during worship, specifically when "praying or prophesying." For most of history, this custom has been followed. Some churches still follow it. Are those churches that do not follow this pattern being disobedient?

To begin with, we can see Paul's specific reason for this instruction in verses five and ten, where the lack of such a covering is described as a sign of disrespect for her husband, who is her head. But this statement of the issue makes it evident that there are really two concepts involved: (1) a woman's respect and submission to her husband as her head, and (2) the sign of this respect. If both of those concepts transcend culture, then the answer to the question would be "Yes."

Considering the first part, it is clear from verses 8 and 9 that it is a part of the creation order, and therefore trans-cultural, that the man is the head of the woman. How this affects the relationship between them is discussed more fully elsewhere in Scripture; for example, in the letter to the Ephesians. In this particular passage, the emphasis is on the woman doing nothing that would question this, which brings us to the second part.

In the culture of that time, it was indecent for a woman to appear in public without a veil, or at least some covering over her head. This is still the case in many parts of the world today. Thus, a woman appearing without this covering would disgrace both herself and her husband. Even if a woman were brazen enough to violate this custom and face scorn on herself, she should not do it because of the disgrace it would bring to her husband.

Paul, himself, seems to refer to this cultural basis for the instruction when he speaks of nature itself teaching this in verses 13 and 14. So we find, within this one passage, a portion of the instruction to be cultural (the covering), and another portion to be trans-cultural (the woman honoring her husband). So then, in those churches which do not observe such a covering, it would not be wrong for a woman to omit it, so long as the omission is not a sign of rebellion against the creation order. On the other hand, in those churches and cultures that still observe the custom, violating it would still be wrong, for the same reason as in Corinth.

There are other instructions in the letters that are culturally conditioned. For example, in several of Paul's letters, he tells the readers to "Greet one another with a holy kiss." That was the customary greeting of a friend in those days. It still is, in many parts of the world. But it would probably be greatly misunderstood in our own culture. There is no impropriety in using a handshake as a greeting in our own culture. Or, among our young people and their popular culture, a "high five" would do nicely.

Another principle which is not often needed, but which would occasionally avoid some wild interpretations is based on the concept of the perspicuity (or clearness) of Scripture. When the writer wrote his message *to* Corinth or Ephesus (or wherever), it was a clear message to those believers to whom it was sent. What those words mean is something that they could understand. Proper interpretation should not assign a meaning that would not be understandable to them.

An example of this is found in 1 Corinthians 13:9-10 (NAS). "For we know in part, and we prophesy in part; but when the perfect comes, the partial will be done away." This verse has been used to teach the cessation of the miraculous gifts of prophecy and tongues, since the New Testament is the perfect revelation that would come. There are valid theological arguments for the cessation of these gifts, but this verse is not among them. The Corinthians had absolutely no idea of a New Testament being assembled. If that is what "the perfect" meant, the words would have been unintelligible to them.

One final caution involves "reading into" Scripture a teaching that is not there, but is rooted in our own presuppositions. There have been some who have interpreted Romans 13:1-7 (NAS) as teaching, not that we should obey our rulers, but that rulers should govern according to God's law. They base this on the assertion that rulers are "ministers of God" (verse 4) and "servants of God" (verse 6). In interpreting this in this way, they ignore the repeated instruction to "be in submission" (verses 1, 5), the repeated warning not to resist (verses 2, 3, 4), and the summary of the passage in verse 7, "Render to all what is due them: tax to whom tax is due; custom to whom custom; fear to whom fear; honor to whom honor." Furthermore, one should always consider to whom the letter was written, or the historical context. In this case, the letter was written to the "beloved of God in Rome, called as saints" (1:7). We have no evidence of any of the Roman rulers of that time being Christians. Paul's instruction could not be addressed to them. Although we could infer that, as servants of God, they should rule in a godly manner, this should be recognized as an inference, not a direct instruction. Even in this, we should be aware of questions as to how we apply this inference to a democratic republic such as our own. (See Chapter Four above.)

Chapter Ten
Behold, He is Coming: The Revelation

The final literary genre of Scripture to be considered is that of apocalyptic writing. This is found in only one book of the Bible: The Revelation, although some passages in Daniel closely resemble it. The word "apocalypse" is derived from a Greek word meaning "uncovering," and comes into our language as a revelation or disclosure.

In our own day, this literary style is not found, although there is superficial resemblance to science-fiction and fantasy. Thus, we can have difficulty in relating to this genre when we seek to learn the truth, which it conveys. In the first centuries of the church, there were other apocalypses circulating, but none of them, of course, is canonical. Contrary to these, it is only in The Revelation to John, as some Bibles entitle it, that we find the truth revealed by our Lord Jesus for the comforting and strengthening of his church through this final age.

Before we consider in depth the apocalyptic form of writing, it would be well to note that The Revelation also contains letters to seven churches in chapters 2 and 3. These letters are somewhat different from the other New Testament Epistles in two respects. The first difference is that the Epistles were written by the inspired writers in their own words, though guided by the Holy Spirit, while these seven letters are dictated directly by the Lord Jesus, with John acting as his recorder. The second difference is found in the content of the messages. The Epistles were written to correct problems in the churches or individuals, or to encourage them, in order that they might more perfectly serve the Lord there and then. They often have a strong doctrinal content. These letters are written to commend and comfort the faithful, and to rebuke and exhort the disobedient. Rather than extensive teaching of the readers, Jesus simply points them to their eschatological hope of final victory and reward.

In spite of these differences, the letters found in The Revelation can be studied using the same principles found in the previous Chapter Nine. In this case, the historical context is particularly important. Reference to a commentary, a Bible dictionary, or a historical reference would be of help in this regard. Beyond this, it should be noted that the pattern of these letters is in perfect accord with the pattern of the rest of the book. Troubles and persecution are coming, but take heart: Christ is in control of all things, and the victorious end is assured.

The apocalypse (for the purpose of this book, we will use the term "apocalypse" to refer to The Revelation exclusive of the letters to the churches.) bears a strong resemblance to the prophetic writings, particularly in its predictive aspect and its use of symbolic language. However, even in these things, there are important differences.

The prophesies were primarily oral. The prophets were sent as God's messengers, usually to the leaders of Israel, to deliver particular messages. These messages were usually delivered verbally. In the prophetic books, these prophesies were recorded and combined with narrative to explain the circumstances to later readers. In contrast, the apocalypse was given to be a written message from the outset, not directed toward any one church leader or group, but to the entire church. This consideration, in itself, leads us to expect a more systematically organized message.

The message of the prophet was usually a warning about some sin of Israel or its leaders. The message of the apocalypse is the certainty of victory, even through persecution. The prediction of the prophet was usually of the punishment of Israel for disobedience, or of the later restoration and blessing of Israel. These were things to happen in history. In the apocalypse, even the future historical happenings are placed in relation to the certain ultimate victory at the end of history.

In the use of symbolic language, the apocalypse strongly resembles prophecy. In fact, some of the scenes described in the Revelation are almost identical to those described by the prophets. For example, the cherubim of Rev. 4:7, 8 are very much like those described by Ezekiel in Ezek. 1:5-9. The imagery of John in the apocalypse is strongly rooted in the Old Testament. Rev. 5:5 speaks of "the Lion of the tribe of Judah," which comes from Gen. 49:9. In the next verse, the image of the Lamb takes us back to the Passover of Exodus. These images were such as the original readers of the book would easily recognize from their knowledge of the Old Testament. Numbers, also are used in a symbolic manner in the apocalypse, particularly the numbers seven, ten and one thousand. A good familiarity with the Old Testament is the best asset the interpreter of the apocalypse can have.

As in all of Scripture, the task of interpretation must begin with proper exegesis. Even in highly symbolic passages, we cannot hope to understand the meaning "for us" until we have determined what the words and grammar mean in their historic and literary context. John was writing to First Century Christians, and his message was intended to be understood by them. We cannot force an interpretation on a word or passage, even on a symbol, that would have been foreign to the minds of the original readers. For example, one book interpreted the two hundred million horses and horsemen (Rev. 9:16-21) as modern cavalry, with the fire and smoke out of the horses' mouths representing the tanks' armament.

This would have been sheer nonsense to the apostle John, himself, as well as to his readers.

The previous example illustrates another necessary aspect of interpretation of the symbolic figures in this book. Just as for prophetic symbols, the details are not intended to be analyzed for their significance. The image is intended to convey a picture in the minds of the readers or hearers. The message is in the picture as a whole, and not in the details. In this case, it is a picture of terrible destruction, by seemingly demonic armies: yet, in verses 20 and 21, the survivors of mankind refused to stop their worship of idols and the demons behind them.

Only when we have determined the grammatical meaning of the passage, are we prepared to find its application to our own situation. In the above example, we are led to realize how easily modern man is led to worship his economic, philosophical and intellectual idols, trusting in them instead of in God. And even when they catastrophically fail, the answer too often is an attempt to fine-tune them and try again.

The best way to avoid the pitfall of getting entangled in the details of the images, which are so common in the apocalypse, is to keep our minds on the overall message of the book. Every portion of the book is contributing to this three-part message: (1)

There will always be trouble and tribulation in this world. (2) Christians will not be immune to this trouble. In fact, in addition to the troubles faced by unbelievers, they will also suffer persecution for their faith. (3) Be of good cheer: Christ has overcome the world and the final victory is certain.

The recognition this central message of the book does not solve all of the hermeneutical problems. It only establishes a sound foundation. How each passage fits into this message is a problem, which still must be faced. There are four main approaches to this problem, each of which has variations. Although they are named for their approach to the millennium (the thousand-year period of chapter 20), they differ in their understanding of how the various passages throughout the book fit into the overall message. We will provide a brief discussion of these schools of interpretation. For those who wish to go into the matter in more detail, a good source of information and discussion is found in "The Meaning of the Millennium: Four Views", edited by Robert G. Clouse, InterVarsity Press, 1977. The book includes a presentation by a spokesman for each of the four schools, with rebuttal by the spokesmen for the other three.

Premillennialism teaches that, at the end of this age, Christ will return with those saints who have been with Him in the intermediate state and will set up his Kingdom over the whole world with the capitol in

Jerusalem. It will be a glorious reign, with the devil immobilized and the entire earth in submission to Christ's perfect justice. In this school of thought, the reading tends to be linear. That is, the various passages of the book tend to be sequential, except for chapter 12. Thus, a vision in chapter 6 will refer to a historical happening that is earlier than one described in chapter 16. There are two main forms of premillennialism: "dispensational" and "historic". These differ widely from each other.

Dispensational premillennialism is part of the broader dispensational theology. In a noble effort to interpret Scripture as God's infallible, inerrant word, this theology is very reluctant to deal with any passage as using figurative language. As a result, prophetic passages, which describe visions in symbolic language, tend to be dealt with literally, even in the details. Because of this, the dispensational contributor to the book cited above declares that Daniel 2:44 predicts this thousand-year reign as a literal earthly kingdom, coming after the conclusion of this Gospel age. But that ignores the beginning of the verse, which declares that this will occur "in the days of those kings". Kings here include Rome and earlier powers even according to dispensational interpreters. Moreover, the verse says, "it [the kingdom] will itself endure forever." But the millennial kingdom will, by the literal description endorsed by these same interpreters, last only for 1000 years, at least in its earthly form as they see it in this prophecy.

This method of interpretation envisions the "rapture" of 1 Thes. 4:16 to occur before the visions of destruction and tribulation found in the apocalypse, although there is no hint of that in the apocalypse. Thus, the major portion of The Revelation is considered entirely future, and its relevance to the Christians of the early centuries is very limited, even though Rev. 1:3 speaks of the blessings to be found by the reader.

The problem with this approach is two-fold. It downplays or ignores the use of figurative language, and it uses Old Testament prophesies to define New Testament interpretation. Of course, one of the main principles of interpretation is that Scripture interprets Scripture. But this principle usually works in the other direction: the more complete revelation of the New Testament gives us light upon the Old Testament passages. In any event, we can see the problems that can occur by ignoring the principles set forth here for interpreting prophetic and apocalyptic passages. Because of these problems, the dispensational method is not used in Reformed circles.

Whereas the dispensational method dates back to the nineteenth century, the historic or classical pre-millennialism is found among the early church fathers, who were much more closely familiar with this genre. They were not reluctant to accept the visions as symbolic images of truth. A beast could be an empire. A woman could be Israel. Much of the truth taught by these images can be found in the Gospels and Epistles. But in the apocalyptic visions, we find the truth in a form which speaks even more directly to the heart. Historic premillennialism differs from post- or amillennialism primarily in seeing the arrangement of the revelation to be in chronological order. Thus, the millennium of chapter 20 must follow the marriage supper and the conquest of chapter 19. Since Christ gathered his people to the wedding supper, and since He came and conquered the nations in chapter 19, the subsequent millennial rule has to be understood as a literal earthly kingdom, following the victorious conclusion of this age, where Christ rules over all the kingdoms of the earth, with his resurrected people assisting Him in that rule.

The amillennial or postmillennial interpreter finds himself somewhat uncomfortable with the concept of saints, in their glorified, resurrected bodies, mingling with ordinary mortals in their fleshly bodies for such an extended period. They note that there is no compelling reason to require that the various visions represent consecutive historical periods. Various proponents of these systems have proposed different historical arrangements, but they all agree that chapter 19 terminates the history of this age and chapter 20 gives us a vision of the entire age, from the resurrection or ascension of Christ to the end of this Gospel age. The binding of Satan (v. 2) is not a complete immobilization, but a restraint, which prevents him from stopping the propagation of the

Gospel throughout this age. The description of 1000 years simply means a long and complete period. All would agree that, during this Gospel millennium, Christ reigns over this earth from heaven by the Holy Spirit through his saints on earth. In this reign, He is joined by the resurrected saints in heaven. And by this reign, He is accomplishing exactly his purpose throughout this age.

The principal difference between the two systems is that the postmillennial interpreter sees a period at the end of the age in which a golden age of spiritual prosperity will be established. Not everyone will be a Christian, but evil will be of small proportions and Christian principles will be the rule. The amillennial interpreter sees this age as one in which both good and evil are advancing. The Gospel message is prospering, but the opposition to it is intensifying. This contrast reaches a climax at verses 20:7-10, which describe the final victory and introduce the final judgment.

From this very brief and necessarily incomplete description of these two schools of interpretation, it is evident that postmillenialism is, in a very real sense, an optimistic form of amillennialism.

Regardless of the method of interpretation used, it is necessary to be aware of the sometimes profound differences between positions held by men of equally sound training and equal respect for the reliability of

Scripture. A proper humility would require that we respect the interpretation given by those of any of the latter three methods of interpretation. In fact, the very existence of these different schools of thought emphasizes the statement of our Westminster Confession of Faith in chapter 1, section 9: "The infallible rule of interpretation of Scripture is the Scripture itself; and therefore, when there is a question about the true and full sense of any Scripture (which is not manifold, but one), it may be searched and known by other places that speak *more clearly*." (Emphasis added.)

Nowhere is this principle more necessary than in the interpretation of prophecy and apocalypse. Visions can bring different concepts to different people. Our interpretation of these symbols must be made in the light of those passages in the Epistles or in the Gospels, which speak in more distinct terms. Reversing this principle and allowing our reception and reaction to the images to color our understanding of the more didactic passages is a dangerous practice. This, indeed, is a fundamental problem with the dispensational approach. However, interpreters of the other schools have largely resisted the temptation to use such an inverted method. As long as we can each receive the apocalyptic message of tribulation, persecution and victory in whatever way the scriptural images persuade us, and leave the formulation of doctrine to the didactic passages, we can truly enjoy sweet harmony in our churches.

Do You Understand What You Are Reading?

One final admonition for effective study of Scripture: Regardless of the genre, or whether the interpretation is simple or difficult, one principle of study is always appropriate: enjoy it!

About the Authors

Ken Pierce graduated from Hillsdale College, Hillsdale, MI in 1993, with a Bachelor of Arts in Religion and History, and in 1996 received the Masters of Divinity Degree from Reformed Theological Seminary in Jackson, MS, where he was a James Henley Thornwell fellow in the department of systematic theology. Having grown up in evangelical congregations of the Reformed Church in America in West Michigan, he began to sense a call to the full-time gospel ministry during his freshman year of college. Desiring to find a denomination true to the beliefs he was taught as a child, he discovered the Presbyterian Church in America. Upon graduating from seminary, Ken completed an internship at the Seventh Reformed Church (independent) of Grand Rapids, MI, and was ordained in the PCA in 1997 while serving as an assistant in that congregation. He pastored the First Presbyterian Church of Greensboro, AL, and the Newbern (AL) Presbyterian Church from 1998-2001. In 2001, he was called as the assistant pastor of the Draper's Valley Presbyterian Church in rural Southwestern Virginia, and in 2003, became minister of that congregation, where he continues to serve. He married his wife, Melissa, in 1996, and they have three children, Abigail, Nathaniel, and Rachel, as well as an irksome hound, Daisy Belle.

Bob Miller holds degrees from Virginia Tech and MIT. Following an industrial career including Vice-President for Engineering, Bob taught at Virginia Tech for 27 years. He was privileged to be involved in the process leading to the establishment of the PCA, having begun his work of churchmanship at the Westminster Church in Roanoke, VA from 1970 to 1980. When the former Reformed Presbyterian Church, Evangelical Synod, began a new church development in Blacksburg, the Millers assisted with that work; Bob served as a Ruling Elder on the Session of Grace Covenant Church, Blacksburg, from 1981 to 1987. Continuing to support church planting, he and his wife joined the work at Harvestwood Covenant Church in Floyd County, Virginia. Bob served as a Ruling Elder in that congregation from 1988 to 2002. A Ruling Elder Emeritus since 2001, the Millers now worship at the Draper's Valley Church in Draper, Virginia where his co-author, Ken Pierce, serves as Senior Pastor. Bob and his wife Beverly, have three grown children, Elaine, Bob and Charles.

www.ingramcontent.com/pod-product-compliance
Lightning Source LLC
Chambersburg PA
CBHW051803040426
42446CB00007B/489